E for Elephant:
Tales of Elephants and Beyond

Madambu Kunjukuttan (1941-2021)

Novelist, Screenplay writer, Actor
Sankaran a.k.a. Kunjukuttan was born (21-06-1941)
after the great cyclone in Kochi to
Sankaran Namboothiri at the Madambu Mana
situated in Kiraloor village in Thalappilly Thaluk.
Expert in elephant science & medicine;
performed priestly rituals.
His creative literary works are
Avikhnamasthu, Bhrashtu, Ashwathdhaamaavu, Enthoru Mahaanu Bhaavalu, Colony, Maraarashree, Poothu, Nishaadam, Saavithridee (A lament), Mahaaprashthaanam, Saadhanalahari, Aathmakadha, Puthiya Panchathanthram, and *Chakkarakkuttippaaru.*
Wife: Savithri (Late)
Two children.
He died of covid-19 on 11 May 2021, at the age of 79.

Story

E for Elephant: Tales of Elephants and Beyond

Madambu Kunjukuttan

Translated by

Rayson K. Alex

Poornima G.

SandDunes

SandDunes

an imprint of green books private limited
gb building, civil lane road, ayyanthole,
thrissur- 680 003, kerala
ph: +91 487-2381066, 2381039
website: www.greenbooksindia.com
e-mail: info@greenbooksindia.com

branches:
thrissur 0487-2422515
thiruvananthapuram 0471-2335301
calicut 0495 4854662

original title in malayalam
a aa aanakkathakal
(story)
by
madambu kunjukuttan

english
e for elephant:
tales of elephants and beyond

translated by
rayson k. alex
poornima g.

published september 2023

cover design : prabhul varma

printed in india
manipal technologies ltd

isbn : 978-93-91072-98-8

₹ 160.00
SDGBPL/05/2023

Contents

Preface

Krishnadas (Late)

Elephants stand apart from other animals owing to the hugeness of their body, the strength and intelligence that these creatures possess. Elephant lovers consider elephants the symbol of prosperity. Elephants play a great role in the cultural and industrial scenarios of Kerala. They are a prominent presence during festivals and in the wood saw-mill factories.

To domesticate wild elephants, humans capture, scare and lure them from the forest. In the process of domesticating the elephants, they are brutally tortured. Even after domestication, they are subject to torture. People who watch the decorated elephants for hours together in temple-festivals, in the context of high-decibel sounds, do not understand the internal conflicts and ordeals that the elephants undergo. They are usually not given sufficient food, rest and medicines. Elephants turn intolerant and temperamental during such situations. The vindictive nature and memory of elephants are well known. Similar to how some elephants that have gained fame through their majestic stature, lovely walk and good behaviour, certain others are notorious for their naughtiness. There are many such stories about elephants. Kottaram Sankunni has given a sacred standing to several elephants in his writings.

In this book, Madambu—famous novelist, pundit of Sanskrit scriptures, a scholar of elephant-science—writes about the poetical history of elephants from memory. Guruvayoor Kesavan, Kavalappara Komban, Poomulli Sekaran are all majestic elephants narrated here. Written in the light of Thirumangalathu Neelakandan Mooss' *Mathangaleela* (a scientific treatise on taming elephants) and Palakappiya Maharshi's *Hasthyayurveda* (The Ayurveda for Elephants), this book will be a novel experience to elephant lovers. ■

Translators Note

Imaging Elephants in Another Tongue

Rayson K. Alex
Associate Professor
Department of Humanities and Social Sciences
Birla Institute of Technology and Science Pilani
K. K. Birla Goa Campus, Goa

The original *A Aa Aana: Aanakathakal* is the experience of cultural elephants who have been domesticated and have been part of the human civilization for centuries. The elephant is a strong-cultural imagery and an icon, a being that people have a strong passion for and an attachment more than fear—no wonder, there are legendary stories about elephants, a science or an Ayurveda about elephants, and a lot of glorification of them. The official animal of Kerala State, elephants have assimilated into the cultural spaces of humans.

There are a lot of rhetoric in the Malayalam language punning on the "concept of elephant." Anything huge can be called an elephant, be it a fat man/woman, a huge building or even a travellers' bus (like the Kerala State Transport buses owned by the government are quite commonly known as "aanavandi" [meaning elephant-vehicle]).

The informal register of the language of the original work in Malayalam is such that the stories are woven with beautiful strings of humour. Though the humour seems to have been lost in translation, the informality of the register in the original are "retained" using common English words and sentence structures, which are often incomplete and awkward. I have given extensive notes in the translated work to clarify certain words, phrases and references to cater to a larger audience, who would otherwise miss the intricacies and nuances of certain usages. I have given a glossary of terms, literary works and Malayalam writers who find mention in the text. Shorter descriptions are added as footnotes.

There are eleven short chapters in the book of which seven are named after legendary elephants in Kerala. The popular names of the elephants known locally are used as titles of the chapters. For instance, "Chengallooraana" and "Kavalappara Komban" stand apart for the use of "aana" (meaning, elephant) and "komban" (meaning, tusker). The first names of all the elephants situate them to a particular place, temple or a family, and thus identify the owners. The nomenclature of "Chengallooraana" shows the cultural elephant-imagination as the "one and only" elephant in the place, referring to its gigantic physical qualities. Kavalappara is a house name, the title of the chapter refers to the masculinity of the elephant. Guruvayoor Kesavan is known as the elephant of the famous Guruvayoor temple. Five chapters out of eleven have a different rationale of nomenclature. The Chapters titled "Nagaradhyakshan" (The Chief of the Elephants) and "Pidikal" (She-Elephants) are about famous mahouts and their extraordinary skills; and she-elephants and their qualities, respectively. The concluding chapter, "Anubhavam" (Experience) narrates the self and others' experience on elephants.

The book is not merely a historic account of elephants in Kerala but also is the socio-cultural imagination of elephants prevalent in the society of Kerala. However, this imagination in many respects is sexist, caste-discriminative, racial and speciestic—sometimes explicit. This hierarchical perspective is the reflection of the society of Kerala that I am much part and aware of. The anthropocentric elephant-imagination is the reflection of the societal imagination of humans and their cultures. However, it is necessary to understand these complexities of relationships and their cultural metaphors as relationships which are not rigid but evolving along with time. These changes are subtly marked in literary, cultural and cinematic expressions of the State. The aforementioned problematic perspective need not blind the readers of this work as it has rich stories of how temple elephants are reared and treated depending on the elephant-imagination of humans. There are debates on elephants in the public sphere about elephant rights, animal ethics and religio-centric approaches to animals. To cite an example, the banning of Elephant Ramachandran in the temples at Thrissur by the Forest Department initiated public dialogues on elephant rights and ethics (https://indianexpress.com/article/india/ban-on-captive-elephant-at-kerala-temple-festivals-triggers-protests-5662859/). The public sentiments of people about the pregnant elephant that died in the river is another example of an elephant story debated by elephant lovers (https://economictimes.indiatimes.com/news/politics-and-nation/pregnant-elephant-dies-after-consuming-pineapple-stuffed-with-crackers-in-kerala/articleshow/76181693.cms#:~:text=A%20pregnant%20elephant%20died%20after,injury%20in%20its%20lower%20jaw.). Such debates and literary works shape the opinions of people about elephants which eventually gets "translated" into the behavioural and perspectival patterns of the public in Kerala.

The process of translation was a learning in itself as I (the translator) had to be in constant contact with the author, Madambu Kunjukuttan. I also had to learn terminologies and techniques from mahouts, Mr. Renju C. K. and Mr. Shanu Vemballi.

This was a translation project awarded to me by the prestigious organisation, Association for the Study of Literature and Environment (ASLE-USA) in 2019 (https://www.asle.org/stay-informed/asle-news/asle-translation-grant-winners-2019/). I thank Prof. Heather Sullivan, Professor of German and Comparative Literature, Trinity University, Texas, and Ms. Amy McIntyre, Managing Director of ASLE, for their constant support and encouragement. I thank Prof. Chia-ju Chang, Professor of Modern Languages and Literatures, Brooklyn College, New York, for her constant encouragement and academic mentorship. Since the volume uses a number of Sanskrit verses from various texts, I had to request Dr. Poornima G., a Sanskrit Professor, to help me with the Sanskrit translation. Thanks to her timely help in translating the Sanskrit texts and also her general advice in the translation of the book. A note of thanks to my dear friends Sachindev P.S., U.A. Manoj, Dr. V. Soba (Editor, Green Books) for helping me with word-meanings and their interpretations. My sincere thanks goes out to Ms. Jyothirmayi Sankaran (sister of Madambu Kunjukuttan) for reading the first draft of the translation for accuracy. Special thanks to my beloved wife, Dr. S. Susan Deborah, for her timely support, encouragement and novel ideas in embellishing this volume. I also wish to thank Mr. Muhammed Irshad Mukkam for sketching the elephants in each chapter of the book, which is a new addition in the translation.

■

Foreword

Spots and Dots on Trunks. The Elephant World Unspeakable

Brigitte Uttar Kornetzky

German-Swiss Filmmaker, Maker of *Where the Elephants Sleep* Founder and President of the Swiss Charity Organization, 'Elefanten in Not' Swiss Ambassador for Captive Elephants, the Federation of Indian Animal Protection Organization in India.

When winged beings sail down from space to earth, it can really only be elephants. And if they land in the trees with their unspeakably heavy weight and break the branches, then perhaps they have sprung from the hands of Brahma. Tradition leaves open what the god actually intended to do with these monstrous, mischievous creatures.

To want to write a book about elephants is like a travel adventure that leads us through the universe of these grey giants. Similar to us humans in many ways, elephants show humour, compassion, self-awareness, playfulness, and also depression. And they are loved, worshipped, feared, hated, tormented, and brutally exploited. Although the object of study by science, and research and countless publications, elephants are and remain, above all, legendary beings who are reluctant to reveal their secrets, or whose secrets we humans have been working on for generations. Elephants show concern for other species and have been known to rescue trapped animals, even not belonging to their own families. The elephant herds are led by matriarchs and thus belong to the closest knot societies in the animal kingdom. Births are major social events, as the cycles of the first-time giving birth females, are often next to one another in short succession.

Many scientists are puzzled about their behaviour, leading to decades of studies, for example, when elephants gather near their dead. A recent review of documented field observations of elephants at carcasses reveals patterns of elephants' behaviour towards their dead, regardless of the strength of former relationships with the deceased individual. The most common behaviours observed were approaching the dead, touching and examining the carcass. This behaviour sends chills up my spine. Would we show reverence to trees illegally mowed down, or towards any dead animal? Would we do this to our forests or lost wildlife? Furthermore, our questions would be, Do elephants generate strength from grief about their dead? Is mourning a common social behaviour that strengthens the community? Do elephants lose these behaviours in captivity? Can we associate temporal gland streaming by a young female standing at her mother's carcass with higher emotions? We lift eyebrows to find out about the motivations underlying observed behaviours but, they are hard to determine. From the ethological and psychological perspective, so many questions remain unanswered while we, at ground level, still have to fight violations and cruelty against elephants.

Elephants fight for their survival as a species, and about their elephant-ness, and against any submission by human hands, be it on tourist rides, safaris, temples, or as working elephants, in zoos, or circuses or at festival sites. Their greatness makes it repeatedly one more time clear again how little, certain sections of the population, understand about them, and perhaps this may be the precise reason for their ruthless treatment by us. What reaches us are stories and observations of encounters between people and the grey giants, with the same question about their relationship. The two-thousand-year-old fable of the six blind men, which the Raja in Savatthi ordered to his court to let them touch the giant animal in order to learn about his being, illustrates an individual approach. The answers couldn't be more different. There was talk of a wall (body), a fan (ears), rope and brush (tail with tassel), and a pipe (trunk), and a column (leg). The impression is literally obvious, science or elephantology is another, seventh being in the great fable about the six blind men who touch the elephant with the question of who they are, not what they are.

The relationship between humans and elephants has existed since time immemorial, when both were still forest dwellers. For half a century this relationship has been subject to rapid change. The picture has changed completely, unfortunately, not for the better. The health and welfare of the elephants have given way to their owners' greed for money and pleasure. The demand from elephants at festivals has skyrocketed and has made Sonepur mela in Bihar the main hub for the elephant trade in India. Too many elephants have been and are illegally caught and 80% of them are illegally brought across the borders from the northeastern states of India. Mismanagement makes elephant husbandry in India appear more than questionable, and casts a long shadow in their future, because the prospect of improvement is only disproportionate to the massive needs of the grey colossi, who wither beyond species-appropriate keeping. In captivity, their high communication skills, their intelligence and their needs in relation to the wild can, in no way, be taken into account.

The giant proboscis are not just eating machines and messy eaters, they are also equipped with the special feature of an excellent memory that remembers its opponents as well as their smallest weaknesses. The use of tools, such as twigs or sticks to scratch, makes us smile again and again, because with it you can get to the otherwise inaccessible parts of the body such as the neck or back. Then the twig is tucked behind the ear like the architect's pencil, and remains ready for use again at any time for both humans and elephants, and the elephant has a free hand again to quickly steal a fruit or vegetable from the bucket when its mahout is turning his back. Often, the question arises about who is studying whose behaviour here.

Elephants. They are the epitome of power, and their majestic beauty should be exaggerated by artists, like painting people, decorating them with colourful cloths, worshiping them like gods in temples and at festivities. This omnipresent animal giant is an indispensable part of the cultural history of India. Kerala alone hosts over 2000 festivals per year, with the temple festival in the Guruvayoor temple in Thrissur being probably the most colourful and the largest; in any case it is a festival in which Lord Krishna is best worshipped, with the greatest number of elephants.

Elephants running amok at festivals like Thrissur leave traces of terror and panic. It is not uncommon for the adored grey giants to have killed ten or more people, mostly mahouts, which does not seem to damage their reputation. Thechikoottukaavu Ramachandran, the biggest temple elephant (10 feet four inches high, 314 centimeters shoulder height) in the South of India, which I was allowed to immortalize in my film with the title *The Elephant Kitchen*, already existed in the years 1988 to 2012 who killed ten people, including five mahouts.

However, no one seems to draw any conclusions from this. Since the musth period of many bulls happens at the same time and falls precisely during the festival season, the increased testosterone level ensures "unleashed" emotions of the animal giants and turns every hierarchy upside down. The elephant dominates the scene; his anger usually discharges at his mahout, who often fails to escape quickly enough to a safe distance, which makes matters worse; because the rage of the left-alone-elephant turns against the next best who stands in the way, even if it is another elephant. I remember a scene in which a frantic bull pushes another elephant from the field with a snort like a bulldozer pushing a pile of earth left behind.

The job of the elephant keeper or mahout today is more like a suicide mission when compared to the honourable profession just a few decades ago, as reflected in this book. Many of the mahouts are underpaid, addicted to alcohol, have unstable private circumstances and only take on such a job because of the few rupees or because no other job can be found; they have no idea about elephant keeping. That is a great disadvantage for both elephants and humans.

If mahouts are known to be the carriers of the stories of their elephants, they still understand little or nothing about their animals. Untutored young men, who lack psychological and biological knowledge, are quick to use violence if the pachyderms don't pay heed, parry or disregard their mahout as a person of respect. The aforementioned frequent change of mahouts also contributes to this. Violence works as a substitute for a non-functioning relationship between the two, the mahout and the elephant, which has been depleted of elephant knowledge. The injuries are mostly fatal to the mahouts, of which there are several hundred every year, across Asia. The stab wounds suffered by elephants from Ankush or the use of knives are deep and heal extremely poorly. If they are not treated medically, which is usually the case, they are excruciatingly painful and sooner or later, also fatal.

While some of the ten thousand people reflexively protect their ears against the exploding fireworks at the lavish festivals in Kerala, sensitive elephant ears have to endure the detonations right next to their ears without reacting. They stand like pillars of salt next to the exploding fireworks, as if they were bursting balloons, at most. It can be assumed that their eardrums suffer severe and painful permanent damage. If the increased testosterone level disinhibits the elephant's unexpected powers, then any restraint or obedience on the part of the animal becomes obsolete. He'll snort everything out of the way that gets in his way.

Thechikoottukaavu Ramachandran, also called Gajakesari, is in the musth for about five long months a year, but he has a good mahout who has looked after him for fifteen years, as also Dr. T. S. Rajeev, Center for Elephant Studies in Kerala, and personal veterinarian of the animal giant. The elephant gives me the horror of my life when it suddenly kneels to the ground about a step away from me. When my gaze carefully climbs up the elephant like a climber on a steep vertical wall, longingly hoping for the end of the wall, I see the huge head of the bull with the clear watery gland towering over me. The gigantic animal, whose head hits the white festival cloud of Kerala, kneels down; cheered by the crowded crowd of his followers, who like to have a few rupees in their pockets to honour their elephant deity. His mahout, thin as a beanstalk, barely reaches his thigh. His foot is just bigger than a single toenail of the grey giant. He holds the ankush in his hand, the front end of which is stuck into the ground with the polished brass point. The fan base of Gajakesari is large and many already gather around the two of them cheering and screaming, with arms stretched high and chanting the rhythm of the drums. The elephant is saddled and decked out for the upcoming procession. As the bearer of the deity, the Gajakesari is undoubtedly the chosen elephant king, and will carry the Idol of God three or more times around the temple center, in whose inner shrine, the sanctum sanctorum called Garbhagraha, Maha Vishnu is venerated. Obviously, its owner has decided not to miss out on the lucrative business and calmly overlooks the potential danger of the "musth-have" condition of his high-earner. From 1922 to 1976 his ancestor, the legendary Guruvayoor Kesavan, to whom a chapter is devoted in this book, took over this role in Thrissur Pooram in his place.

Many mahouts and elephant owners decide against any precautionary measures in parading their elephants even though they are in musth. This irrationality has its price, however, and usually ends fatally. A king has the right to kill. And the king is the elephant, as Mathangaleela puts it, whose reading means something like elephant sport or elephant games. The life of a mahout or even a helper is worth next to nothing in Kerala. Elephant insurance companies provide clear information about this. A dead elephant is worth more than a live one. There are no penalties and the insurance sums are high. Lessons are also drawn, and ethical values are obsolete. It is part of the big business with the giant animals. Good mahouts are rare these days. Bad or with no payment at all, the mahouts constantly switching to other elephants, whose owners promising higher payments at the beginning, increase the risk of accidents. In addition, there is a lack of knowledge about the animals and the constant consumption of alcohol by the keepers, which makes it impossible to establish a good and lasting relationship between the mahout and the elephant.

This additional stress is excruciating for the animals, due to the generally high testosterone level. Some elephant bulls react with lethargy (possibly drugged for safety to humans), however, with others an unpredictable and dominant, even aggressive behaviour is observed. Only a few mahouts are allowed to tie their elephants in the forest during the musth period. The assistants then tied the elephants' front legs tightly together (hobbled), and the long chain was attached to the animal's back leg. The elephants hop through the forest and can be quickly tracked down due to the long chain. The freedom of movement for the elephant animals in the musth is less than that of a duck in a pond. Nobody, except the animal rights activists, regards this stress of the animals as cruelty to animals. Nevertheless, elephants chained in the forest show less aggressive behaviour during the musth period than elephants at parades and festivities, since they are isolated in a calm and natural environment. They are much more relaxed in the forest.

Post-traumatic stress disorders can be observed in almost all elephants in captivity; it is the stereotypical bobbing and swaying, a misconduct, and a sure sign of the lack of freedom of movement of elephants in captivity which incidentally could never be observed in wild elephants. For wild elephants, being locked in captive conditions, means a lifelong, never-ending trauma after the break-in. Exiled into slavery to give their best to fulfil the human benefit that we have imposed on them, the "domesticated" elephants degenerate into a shadow of their former wild glory. The elephants in captivity are literally going insane or become lifeless robots.

In the course of their more than 3-4,000 year history of development, elephants have not left their wild life-status, even when they are born and grow up in human custody. They have never been domesticated like cattle, horses, cats, or dogs; their generations have not been modified to serve any particular human purpose. Condemned to spend the rest of their lives in chains, fear and terror, above all a life in solitary confinement and prison in zoos, temples or on private property, in which they are forced to earn their living and that of their owners. They have to work in tourism in Jaipur or in timber hauling in Kerala under inhumane conditions. They are ghettoized, kept in solitary confinement, tortured and condemned to a life in chains.

Young elephants, as young as five years old, are broken into, which means that after they are captured from the jungle, they are tortured and humiliated in a kraal (called phajaan in Thailand) for between six and twelve days until they give up exhausted, and collapse. From then on, they will be exposed to lifelong human abuse. This panic and fear of further agony caused by people or the mahout, who alternately torments him and then saves him from further agony by giving him food and water again to lead him out of the kraal, forces even the strongest elephant for all future into abject obedience; unless he is, perhaps, in the musth and opposes humans. How does such subservience of the elephants, who absolutely want to avoid any further infliction of pain, behave with that half of the brain of the animal that previously (before the break-in) could easily assert itself in the wild? Elephants are exposed to this permanent initial trauma, which is followed by countless numbers in the course of their life in captivity, which is usually far too short. The current system of elephant-keeping, unfortunately, hardly allows innovative changes. It is hardened, stubborn and corrupt. With its lack of understanding and mismanagement, it finally brings many elephants into the grave prematurely, especially bulls that are just 30 or 40 years old.

There are two standard works in Indian elephantology that are frequently mentioned in this book. The Hastyayurveda, with its over one hundred and seventy-one chapters (171) and in it occurring 12,000 verses or slokas, also called shoklams, in which the author Sage Palakappya deals with the characteristics of elephants and their diseases such as fever, relating to their eyes, teeth, etc. as well as the trapping and taming of wild-caught animals, and the diagnosis and application of Ayurvedic medicine. It is divided into four major sections as follows: 1. Maharogasthanam, 2. Kshudrarogasthanam, 3. Sallyasthanam and, 4. Uthrastanam. The hour of birth of the elephants is ascribed in *Hastyayurveda* to the two hands of Brahma, who holds a cosmic egg in his left hand, from which seven male elephants are born, and from his right hand seven female elephants arise.

The *Mathangaleela*, recorded by Neelakanta, an ancient book frequently mentioned by the author, seems to be the basis of the author of this book's willingness to associate. In the translation of Jacob Cheeran's Sanskrit into Malayalam, this standard work of the then elephantology was made available to the general public in Kerala and has since gained popularity. The *Mathangaleela* with its 12 chapters and around 253 stanzas is said to be 200 years old, but is often assigned to an even older period, as the elephants were thought to have the ability to fly.

This myth, at first a curse, which in turn became a curse during the Enlightenment, brought them together with their weight to earth in order to serve humans from then on. Due to the accessibility of this work to the general public in Kerala, the traditions, in spite of modern knowledge, ignore species-appropriate housing conditions for the giant animals, and seem even to have hardened against modern scientific findings. The division of elephants, a Schedule 1 animal (of the Wildlife Protection Act 1972) of the wild animals, into castes not only seems outdated, it seems to a certain extent, also out of place in the case of elephants or has been assigned differently. As an extended arm of some popular traits, as they are known for example in horses, cattle or dog breeding, it seems to find an excessive application here, for instance elephants are preferred if they have long legs (deer caste), or nicely coloured, speckled points on the trunk or the forehead. If at all the trunk and the tail are long with a pronounced tassel and the tusks are well formed and powerful (manda caste), or the profitable shoulder height puts all smaller elephants in the shade or eliminates them. The valuation of an elephant rises and falls with the criteria similar to an exhibited cow in a cattle fair or a mela. The price drops dramatically when the animal giant is one-eyed, deaf, and has bad manners, only half an ear or only one tusk.

Bhadra caste, manda caste, deer caste, mixed caste find correspondence in the castes of the Brahmins, the very heroic Kshatriyas, the ruling class, Vaishyaas and the Shudras, the lowest caste, to which artists and workers are assigned to serve the first three higher-ranking castes. The Brahmins were allowed to farm and raise livestock, whereas the Vaishyaas were mostly merchants who traded in agricultural products or breeding. These four castes are mentioned in Mathangaleela. However, there is not such a thing as a caste for elephants that they would assign to themselves. This was just another way of "humanizing" elephants. Genealogically, however, the interesting question remains why the caste system was used with the elephants. Was it due to their intelligence?

The striking proboscis have moved the human imagination for millennia. Elephas Maximus Indicus and Loxodonta Africana are the result of more than 50 million years of evolution, and we have only just begun to study and understand their behaviour and role in an endangered ecosystem.

Keeping elephants in the service of earning a living in the broadest sense cannot be maintained in this way. Too much is at stake, too many elephants are constantly dying from the consequences of the most miserable housing conditions, especially in Kerala, but also in other states, and the species as such is listed on the IUCN's list of endangered species. Their massive, primeval appearance has not stopped us humans from enslaving and subjugating them. We brought them to the brink of extinction by breaking their will to live, destroying their habitat, and treating them for life as our subjects, who are often worthless than a piece of dirt. Elephants are not breeding animals, it has to be explicitly mentioned again that they are wild animals, even if about 2675 elephants are currently living in captivity in India (as of the Ministry of Environment and Forest & Climate Change (MoEF & CC) information to the Supreme Court (SC) in 2019), and breeding has been tried often enough; it can be described as a failure. Elephants have until today, not been domesticated.

So it is up to us, humans, whether and how we want to handle the story, once begun by gods and orphans, demystified, to our descendants and continue to tell. In favour of a respectful and life-affirming ecology of elephants and humans, which puts the preservation and protection of the natural habitat of these giant animals at top priority, our concern must be about the management and conservation of these last and largest mammals on our planet. As keystone species, elephants shape and modify the habitat in favour of other species with which they share their habitat. Experiencing and studying elephants in the wild is like a spiritual experience that will captivate one for life and that never ends as long as elephants are among us.

Elephants are hunted and shot by the thousands every year for their ivory, caught in traps, run over by trains, electrocuted by high-voltage wires, and lose their lives through poaching and untreated diseases in captivity, poisoned in retaliation and deprived of their habitat by people encroaching their forests. The entire elephant families have witnessed such mutilations. We can assume that these mutilations are deeply engraved in their collective memory, similar to us humans. At this point, we should be aware that just a few decades ago neither African nor Indian societies drastically decimated elephant herds or other wildlife species through hunting and thus brought them to the brink of extinction. The conflict between humans and elephants is already raging as a conflagration if the illegal exploitation of resources in the elephant areas is not prevented.

We will not be able to undo what is broken, but we can stop to continue inflicting cruelty to elephants by understanding their ancient social bonds and behaviour and our relation within, the very moment we stop inflicting cruelty to ourselves. We should accept elephants as equal beings as well as giraffes, dolphins, whales and other species that are allowed to claim a right to their habitat. We should all open our eyes, so to speak, as the seventh unit—to paraphrase the fable of the six blind men—studying, exploring, protecting and enjoying this wonderful being. We're just a heartbeat away from extinction.

Let us hope this book will once again cause us all to stand up for these battered, fabled beings. In the 21st century, with all its challenges in terms of climate and species protection, increasing epidemics, and thus a rapidly increasing risk of losing the delicate balance on this planet in a very short time, elephants in captivity should disappear from the scene in India once and for all. This hope of the MoEF & CC in India in relation to the 103 elephants in Jaipur should be emphasized. With losing the elephant herds living in the wild, we lose the elephants inside us, just as the colonization and destruction of indigenous peoples has already caused irreparable disturbance in us. That destruction shaped our behavioural patterns as well as that of the elephants and is anchored in our cultural memory as well as in that elephant memory that once knew how to fly.

We wish everyone a safe and inspiring journey, and a happy landing while reading this dazzling book.

Ahimsha. ■

E for Elephants:
Tales of Elephants and Beyond

This is not an elephant-story; yet it is as well

This is not a myth; yet it is as well.

This is not science of elephants, yet it is as well.

So,

This is this…

Madambu Kunjukuttan

Chapter 1

Chengallooraana

(The Elephant of Chengalloor)

Engaanum thellilakkam thava varikililee!
Mattoraadhaaramillii
Njangalkkonnaayurappoodamaruka, phanamo-
Raayiramkondumoppam.
Mangaathe thaangi ninniiduka bhujagapathee!
Bhuumiye thumganaakum
Chengalloore gajeendran dharaniyiladhunaa
Sanjarikkunnu mandam.

- Mahakavi Oravangara

Oh Earth! Stand firmly,
a little movement may render us supportless.
Oh, the Lord of snakes (Anantha)!
Be careful to bear the earth motionless
With the aid of your thousand strong hoods
(to prevent the possible earthquake)
Likely to be caused by the huge and
tall elephant of Chengalloor
who is slowly marching forward.

(Trans. Poornima G.)

There has never been such an elephant in Kerala and Thrippunithura, and will never be." (These lines have been blessed by Kottarathil Sankunni).

Eleven feet height (some say 11.25). Matching body length, sizeable weight and beautiful colour—the King of Elephants—all the best qualities come together for Ranganathan. Today, the tallest elephant is only 10 feet or so. He is one foot taller. This is worthy of mention. On seeing this wonder, the great poets used all their imaginative skills to write poems about him. Purazhiyam Valiya Raman Elayath and Vallathol, the male avatars of the goddess of knowledge, wrote about Chengalloor elephant. When the majestic Chengalloor Ranganathan stood on the temple grounds touching the clouds slowly moving his ears rhythmically, inside the walls of the temples, the poets and the *rasikas*[1] adored the four-lined, metrical poems in Sanskrit.

From the time of the *Vedas*, people took care of elephants. Elephants were used to lessen the physical effort of humans, fight against armies, and display richness and ornamentation. The kings used elephants as vehicles. A ride on an elephant is a light adventure for tourists. The Sanskrit word for elephant in Rig *Veda* is "ibham." We do not know when humans would have begun celebrating festivals. When the hunter-gatherers settled for agriculture, they would have begun celebrating their yield. But hunting-festivals would have begun way before. After the stomach, the heart has to be full. Food is for the nutritional needs of the body. Then, we "have" festive celebrations for the mind. From the gambling of the Kings, to the game of cricket that the nations play, all are meant for entertainment, aren't they? This is for a timepass. Sorry, but elephants are not for entertainment.

And Chengalloor elephant is not an entertainment, whatsoever. The tallest elephant that humans have ever domesticated! We

1. In Indian classical canon, *rasikas* are the aesthetes who have in-depth knowledge about art.

do not have elephants that are 10.5 feet, nowadays. No one will believe that he was eleven and more feet. Many of them cannot agree on his height. I am talking about people who are so good at calculations. But they will also agree on the height of Chengalloor elephant. And yet, some say that the Chengalloor elephant is the second tallest; they say the first was another one. If you ask, "which one was that?", they would fumble to say, "but it was there." Human nature, that's all I can say.

Recently, I heard that the skeleton of Chengalloor elephant which is exhibited in the Thrissur Museum does not completely belong to him. This means that some bones belong to some other elephant. Because all the bones could not be retrieved, it seems, …Oh, my goodness! No words to utter. That's a Malayali[2] mind.

That's that. Let's keep aside all of these approximations, jealousy and gossips. The truths that I know, I shall say. Chengalloor Namboothiri bought this elephant from Sreerangam in 1905 for Rs. 1500. Those days it was a huge amount. The entire Kaanjaani Kantassam (two neighbouring villages in Trichur district) Kadavu (reference to a large mass of land) could be bought with that amount. And yet, Namboothiri went all the way to Sreerangam to buy the elephant. Never have I heard that an elephant was bought in Chengalloor before or after. Chengalloor elephant was bought in 1905. In 1914, Aghori Govindan stabbed Chengallooraana. In 1917, Chengalloor Ranganathan attained *moksham*. Chengallooru Namboothiri, who was a landlord, never bought an elephant anytime later. An elephant! A divine reason! A miracle in the history of elephants. Never heard of such an elephant in India from the period of Vedas. Nowadays, there are no elephants without being bestowed with the honour of "King of Elephants" in Kochi and Central Malabar.

It is during the Arattupuzha temple festival *(Pooram)* that Ranganathan was stabbed by the co-elephant. I have heard that

2. People who speak the Malayalam language are called Malayali (People who belong to the Southern State of Kerala are called Malayali [plural: Malayalikal or Malayalees]).

Aghori Govindan was a disgraceful elephant. The places where it steps would perish. Now let me tell you, years have passed even after Govindan expired. The hearsay about the iron-strength of the elephant was disbelieved. The attribution of the iron-strength to that elephant is maybe because he stabbed the King of Elephants—Chengallooraana. How could he murder the gracious Chengallooraana! May not be in his good senses. Due to the stress of musth and the search for a she-elephant, Govindan would have unknowingly stabbed thinking of Ranganathan to be his enemy who came in between he (Govindan) and his she-elephant. The hightide of heat-stress! However, we do not have the right to judge Govindan as a murderer. But cannot forget that he was the reason for the death of *Chengallooraana*.[3] Mr. *Chovvalloor Krishnankutty*[4] once wrote "Akavoor Govindan was the incarnation of Dignity, who doesn't care, come what may." (This is written in the "Preface" to the volume *Paarameekkaavvu Sree Parameshwaran*[5] written by Mr. C. A. Menon, who can be qualified as Elephant-Menon[6] [*Aana* Menon].)

Sreeranganathan, who misrouted from Lord Devendran's herd of elephants (Gajayoodham) returned home six years ago.[7] Yet, people speak about him as if they witnessed his solemn procession carrying the idol in the last year's temple festival. People who are crazy after elephants, talk as if they saw him seconds ago. There is only one reason for all these, that is, his stature. There are no other stories about this noble elephant. But only once he met with an accident. It is the story of Ranganathan

3. The suffix, *aana* in the name Chengallooraana means "elephant."
4. Chovvalloor Krishnankutty is a lyricist for Malayalam films and a journalist.
5. This book is named after the iconic elephant Parameekkavvu Sree Parameswaran.
6. In the sense that he knows the ins and outs about elephants.
7. The imagery of "Devendran's herd of elephants" implies that Sreeranganathan is a heavenly being.

rescued from a marshy pond that he accidentally fell into. It was indeed a Himalayan task, those days. Nowadays, the assistance of machinery is common. Today, there are "iron elephants[8]" like JCB and Hitachi that can lift anything from anywhere as long as it has a firm ground to fix its "legs." Iron hands! With ease, these iron-butterflies can do any work. Today, it can just lift the Chengallooraana with its long "trunk." That's today! But those days, it was only the human effort. There are no machines that are as powerful and flexible as the hands of humans that made huge pyramids and the sky-piercing temple *gopurangal*.[9]

Elephant experts say that there are no elephants beyond the height of an elephant goad. Less than four *kols* (1 *kol* is equal to 72 centimeters). This is the common law. But Chengallooraana broke the rule. His height was the reason for bringing him from Sreerangam, to Chengalloor Illam. In Sreerangam, he was one of the temple-dwellers, taking care of some of the religious duties. As he was growing taller and taller it was difficult for him to pass through the *gopuram* doors. How much ever he bows down his head and spine, he would scrape his skin and break his shoulderbone. So, the temple officials sold him. To fetch holy water for the deity Sreeranganathan[10], a small elephant will be better. He can carry the Amrutha pot and reach anywhere. The deity did not want to see the black warriors in pain. That's what Sreerangathappan[11] likes.

---

8. Reference to earthmovers punning on the size of elephant. JCB and Hitachi are companies that are known for making earthmovers like excavators and tractors.

9. Pyramidal tower usually seen at the entrance of temples in South India. *Gopurangal* is the plural form and *gopuram* is singular.

10. Sreeranganathan is the residing deity of the Sri Ranganathaswamy Temple in Sreerangam. He is an avatar of Lord Vishnu.

11. Depending on the affection and imagination of the devotees, they call the deity by different salutations. One such salutation is Sreerangathappan (*Appan* means father; so, the interpretation could be Sreeranganathan, our father.)

After he reached Kerala, he began growing faster. They say one gets taller by adding inches on to the body, one by one. He was given palm trees and cool water. Minute by minute he grew. Became fatter. Became healthier. He was the one who carried the idol always and everywhere.

But Akavoor Govindan arrived to injure him who was carrying the idol, holding his head high, touching the sky. Everybody knows that Govindan has the habit of attacking the elephants in the line during the festival. So they were always cautious. The mahout of mahouts, popularly known as Paroli, was on the elephant as well. Yet, he stabbed Ranganathan and Ranganathan fell on the ground. The innocent Ranganathan who came from the land of the Pandyas did not know how to quarrel.

Chengallooraana was an innocent being, a famed one too. That need not be separately told. Even after nearly hundred years of his passing, the fame of Sreeranganathan attracts the elephant lovers. Though they say, "Small is beautiful," the principle does not apply to everything. Small might be beautiful. But big is great, we know. Vilangankunnu[12] is beautiful. But the greatness of the Himalayas cannot be attributed to it. The bigness in sight attributes greatness. Anything that is extraordinary possesses divinity. Such things are graceful as well. Everyone knows that beauty contests are so peripheral. And yet, we fold our hands to the beauty queens in respect. Even if Chengallooraana had no physical greatness, he would be loved by everyone.

Here, it is not only about image. I have heard that Chengalloor Ranganathan was well-behaved as well. Whatever it may be, an elephant is a wild animal. But often considered a domestic animal. Every elephant is first an Ayyappan[13]. They are brought from the forest to the human world. Elephants are unlike cows, dogs or pigs. They have lived with humans for generations.

12. Reference to a hillock in Adat panchayat near Thrissur.

13. One who wishes to see the deity the very first time.

Without humans, the dogs wouldn't exist. Elephants are an exception. As elephants have advanced brains and huge physical stature, they have to be loved and inflicted pain to acquaint them with human civilization. So, it is difficult to know their real behaviour. It is after a long association with elephants that we can get to know their behavioural patterns. That's it. Their behaviours are unpredictable. An elephant that behaved itself can be mischievous in the 21st year. Those who are well-versed in elephant safety (Gajarakshathanthra) might not understand their psychology.

We have many elephant stories. Stories of mahouts as well. Elephants are known after the names of their owners. Owners are known by the elephants also—for instance, Chengalloor Ranganathan's mahout. That is a matter of pride. The naughty one was trained by the famous Kadalayi[14] Namboothiri. That is also a pride for elephants. There is only one elephant that is known for himself, his owner, and his mahout alike. He is Ranganathan. In that case, you might ask, "how about Guruvayoor Kesavan?" That's another story. You cannot mix the stories of humans with the stories of the world-renowned Guruvayoorappan. Sriguruvayoor Appan's elephant is Guruvayoorappan himself.

14. Kadalayi is a place near Kannur.

Chapter 2
Guruvayoor Kesavan

Maarthaandasyayatho/ndhathojanirabhudu
Bhrahmarshibhirdarsitham
Sandeeptham kila thathkapaalayugalam
Paanidwayeena daraathu
Sapthaagaayadajaha pragruhyayugapath
Saamaanyathairaavatho
Naagoobhudatha saptha vaaranavaraa
Jaathaaha prudhggaanathaha
(*Mathangaleela,* Pradhamasargam, Shlokam 22)

From which ovum the sun was born and further bifurcated into
A pair of shining bones was shown to Brahma by Brahmarshis[15].
With due respect, Brahma held these shining bones
With his two hands simultaneously and sang the 'Sama'[16] seven times,
The elephant 'Airaavatam[17]' was born first, followed by
The other seven elephants from each of the song.
(Trans. Poornima G.)

---

15. Brahmarshi is the member of the Sages who are believed to have composed the *Rig Veda*.
16. *Vedas* of melodies and chants in the Hindu Scriptures are called Sama.
17. Airaavatam is a mythical tusker who is the vehicle of Lord Indra.

Among the eight elephants that were formed, Airaavatam was the noblest of all. Guruvayoor Kesavan belongs to the lineage of Airaavatam.

There are no elephants on earth that are as famous as Guruvayoor Kesavan. There are no organisms on earth as divine as Kesavan. Though he died, his fame has no death. Perhaps, a wild animal has gained more fame than any human being on earth. Yes, a wild animal. An elephant is the son of the forest. Every elephant is new and different. A divine animal that has not been touched by the smell of humans.

Even though elephants have been domesticated for over 1000 years, they are considered wild. Though the original home of cows, and dogs, is the forest, elephants did not give birth and flourish along with humans. There are also other domestic animals that "traditionally" tend to share cultural spaces with humans. For them the forest is a distant, old story. Even without memories, an unseen connection can be drawn. How about elephants? These wild beings have been trapped and caught from the forest to forcefully adapt to human culture. Every elephant is new, modern and pure.

That could be the reason why elephant psychology is difficult to learn. We can, more or less, understand the behaviour of domestic animals. There is no tested method to identify the mood swings of elephants. When wild elephants are domesticated and brought to live with humans, they reflect what they learned from humans-merely obeying, fearing torture. Like other animals, they could also demonstrate fear and anger. Like cattle, for instance. If we pay attention to the anger, we could learn the nature of elephants. With a daily acquaintance with the elephant we can identify if they will move out, confront or will stab a co-elephant. The smell of the fluids secreted from elephants indicate many things. One needs to be careful. Very careful. The smell of the secretions *(madajalam)* during musth is different. But no one including the mahout and the owner, invest time to learn it. Neither do they want to learn it now.

Such partial knowledge is enough! Torture. Torture as much. To unchain the elephant, particularly during musth, the mahouts use severe torture methods. This is the commonly practiced norm. We do not know why such cruel methods are adopted in chaining and unchaining, particularly during this season. It is like a contract between the elephant and the mahouts. After the elephant passes the musth season, it should remember this torture until the next year; that is the idea.

We will think about the torture methods later, now, it is the story of Kesavan. On the 14th of January, 1922, Mahadevan Thampuran in the Nilambur Kovilakam brought the elephant to the Guruvayoor Temple. Even the Nilambur Kovilakam was looted during the notorious and dreadful mutiny of Mappila. Along with other looted goods the elephant was also stolen. Knowing that Kesavan had been stolen, not only the family but the entire kingdom panicked. Fear was the common feeling of the place. The damage due to the mutiny adversely affected the Hindus. Large number of people belonging to the Namboothiri and Nair castes fled from Malabar to Kochi. Even during Tipu's reign people fled in fear of the army. Many Hindus were forced to wear the Muslim Topi and converted to Islam. Because of the memory of the previous deadly conflicts between the Hindus and the Muslims, the Malabar Hindus fled the place to stay alive. It was during this time that Kesavan was also stolen. The eldest mother Thampuraatti[18] could not bear the grief of Kesavan being stolen. She believed that the grace of the family was stolen. An ardent devotee of Lord Guruvayoorappan, she submitted all her grief to him. In her mind, it seems, she felt comforted and thus believed that Guruvayoorappan will bring back Kesavan without any harm. She also promised Guruvayoorappan that if Kesavan comes back she will offer him to the temple.

18. The wife of an elder Brahmin is called a Thampuraatti. The Brahmin is addressed as Thampuraan. It also denotes a hierarchical order as the words are used by lower castes. Kings are also called Thampuraan.

Guruvayoorappan heard the prayers of the mother Thampuraatti. When the mutiny subsided, an unknown mahout brought Kesavan back to the Kovilakam, saving him from the looters. No one knows who that outsider was, where he came from or where did he leave to. Some elderly believers said that the unknown person was the Guruvayoorappan himself. Whoever that was, Kesavan returned. Baby Krishna who saved Poonthanam[19] disguising as Mangattachan[20] could also disguise as a mahout.

It is that adolescent-tusker Kesavan who became world-known, synonymous to Guruvayoorappan, and graced people on all occasions. This is not loose talk. Seeing Kesavan was like the divine sight of Guruvayoorappan. This great Ganapathi, while he young, was notorious for being wanton and hysterical. While he was a boy he was often agitated. He turned out to be a mature, well-behaved elephant after he was trained once and had drunk holy water from the temple well. The two mahouts, Achuthan Nair and Mani Nair, are to be remembered at this moment. Their contributions have helped in moulding the personality of the elephant.

Gajashasthram says that mature elephants have the intellect of a five-year old human child. They have good memory. We do have a lot of such experiences. The great poet, Vyloppilli's famous poem "Sahyante Makan"[21] (Son of Sahya Ranges) is about a she-elephant's memories. The poem is based on the experience narrated by Therambil Sankunni Menon, a forester by profession. During that time, the kingdom of Kochi was ruled by Madakshi Theesan. He trapped a she-elephant. While lifting her from the elephant-pit[22], her trunk got injured. The

19. The story of Poonthanam and Mangattachan can be read here: http://guruvayurstories.blogspot.com/2010/07/poonthanam-and-mangattachan.html

20. Name of a person.

21. The translation of the poem can be accessed here: https://sonofsahyaranges.wordpress.com/

22. Elephant pit is made to trap elephants for domestication.

forest officials nursed the injury by giving her necessary medicines and care in the best way they could. Once she started getting better, the Thampuran ordered: "Release the young she-elephant in the forest." Half-minded, the foresters obeyed the command. Years passed by. Therambil Sankunni Menon got transferred to many places. Before retirement, he visited Malayathoor again. Summer season. As he had to stay back that day, he slept on the veranda of the office. Deep slumber. In the midnight, he felt a hand gently rubbing his body. In the moonlight, he knew that the hand was the trunk of an elephant. He patted the trunk with his hand. He felt the scar of a dried injury.

"Is that you, my daughter!"

The she-elephant that he had nursed and given medicinal decoction many years ago had returned to see the father.

Elephants remember people who loved them and also those who had inflicted pain on them. They don't forget love and violence. Modern Zoology might not agree with this. Experience. Self-experience! There is no rule beyond it. How many stories would elephant-owners, mahouts and lovers have to tell! When Guruvayoor Kesavan is a legend, there wouldn't be any dearth of stories.

All animals display four kinds of behaviours (castes). In old Malayalam we may categorize it as 1. Brahmana-Kshatriya-Vaishya-Shoodra, 2. Mixed castes, 3. The primitives and so on. Traditional farmers know which bull is lazy while ploughing the field, which one destroys the cattleshed and which one brings disgrace. This is a long-drawn knowledge acquired through experience. This is what evolves into science. Sage Palakappiyan lived 12000 years with elephants. That's how he learned the food preferences, mood swings, and behavioural patterns of elephants (*Mathangaleela*, 19th Shlokam, The Life of Palakappiyan).

There are lovely stories about the love affairs of Kesavan. Radha and Lakshmi. They are the girlfriends of

Guruvayoorappan. There were many viewers who were horripilated by the sight of the romantic revelry of the elephant lovers, Ambady Kannan (reference to Lord Krishna) and Radha, in the context of the song of Ashtapathi[23]. Kesavan had attained the status of an extraordinary, sacred animal during that time. Devotees could not believe that he is a four-legged animal. Though he quarrelled at times, he never hurt anyone. This is not quarrel in dispute but quarrel to join. Initially, he was sent to the factories for lifting felled tree-logs. There, he quarrelled and walked to Guruvayoor. He never quarrelled on the way. Did not destroy anything as well. But there was an air of fear created as he walked. On the command of the district collectors, there were policemen ready with their loaded guns to shoot him, if needed. Even now people narrate the thrilling stories of his elopement. The story of Kesavan who set out to Guruvayoor from the timber factory owned by Ezhuthupurackal Raghava Menon giving a scare to Achuthan Nair and Mani Nair. He is Guruvayoor Kesavan. Crazy boy. Now in his musth as well. Creating minor losses in the timber factory, set out to Guruvayoor. Spat the strong coir that is used to carry timber, lifting his head and tail, as if ready for a battle, he turned back, then walked forward, without turning back. He walked through the main road. Like the spectacular procession of the king. The King of Elephants reached Thrissur via Chalakudy and Olloor. Roamed in the Thekkinkaadu Maidaan (the open ground situated in the heart of the Thrissur city) and bathed in the river. By this time, the guns and policemen had arrived. There were no tranquilizer guns those days. Only gun shots to kill. What if Kesavan, the avatar of Guruvayoorappan, had to be shot? Fortunate! Kesavan reached Manajulal (the famous banyan tree in the east side of the Guruvayur Temple; Manjula is the great devotte of Guruvayoorappan and 'aal' means Banyan tree) without hurting anyone on the way. He bestrides

---

23. Translated as Song of Govindan (Gita Govindan) composed by the 12th century poet Jayadeva.

the cow named Radha and her calf who were lying across the road. Radha, the cow, also belongs to Guruvayoorappan. Shrinking his body, he got inside through the north *gopuram* of the temple, walked auspiciously to the south part and stood in elegance. Now, anyone can tie him. There is no need to chain him. That's Kesavan!

I can go on writing about Kesavan. Unnikrishnan Puthoor has written a monograph on the Gajarajan,[24] *Guruvayoor Kesavan*. M. O. Joseph made a film on Guruvayoor Kesavan. The film was scripted by Unnikrishnan Puthoor. P. Bhaskaran penned the lyrics. Stories and essays on Kesavan were produced. There were even TV serials produced on Kesavan, but not the complete History of Kesavan. His stories are being retold with surprise and reverence among Malayali communities across the world. People knew Kesavan through the life-throbbing photographs clicked by the world-famous photographer, Pepita.[25] One of her photographs of Kesavan will soon be printed as a postal stamp by the Indian Government; this is approved in principle.

The divine transfiguration of Kesavan equalled his life as an avatar of Guruvayoorappan. On the dawn of *Ekadashi naal*[26], while listening to the shlokas of *Narayaneeyam* (authored by Veda Vyasa), the gajaraja looked at Guruvayoorappan, left his body, passed through the North Gopuram, circumambulated the holy place, stepped inside the sanctum sanctorum and merged in Sri Guruvayoorappan.

---

24. The King of Elephants.

25. Pepita Seth is a British photographer whose photographs of Guruvayoor Kesavan made her famous. She was honoured with Padma Shree in 2012.

26. The eleventh day of the lunar month.

Chapter 3
Kirangaattu Kesavan

Vimshathya nakhasamkhyayaanjithapadaha
Spharoonnathiha kumbhayoo-
Rachidraanjalarakthakarnnayugalaha
Sushlakshna kakshaha karii
Savyaathyunnathamaukthikadyuthiradaha
Samboornakukshiha krama-
Sphularjwayathachaarubaaladhikaraha
Pugeephalashyaamalaha
(*Mathangaleela,* Dwithiasarggam, Shlokam 3)

Four uniform legs with twenty nails on the feet,
A pair of tall and huge cranium
Wide ears with red-coloured edges without
any wear or tear and fleshy armpits
Big and pearl-like shining right tusk,
characteristic complete belly (abdomen),
Beautiful straight tail thick at the beginning
gradually leaning downwards, long
And beautiful trunk, dark in colour similar
to the dark blue colour of the *Poogiphalam*[27]
(These are the essential features of an ideal tusker)
(Trans. Poornima G.)

---

27. This is a fruit that belonged to an ancient Kerala. The author of the book has not seen it. It would have got extinct. However, the colour of the fruit is similar to the *njaaval*/Jamun fruit (Indian blackberry; *Syzygium jambolanum*).

Oh yes! The certainties of the masters. Not over, more to follow. The sage narrates the qualities of an elephant to be adorned as the King's vehicle and the qualities of a warrior elephant. The book of *Mathangaleela* is an abridged version of the great work, *Hasthyayurveda* (Elephantology) written by Palakapya Maharshi.

Muneendrodithamaathanga-
Shaasthragaadhaarnavaanmayaa
Alpaamaathangaliileethi
Labdheeyam shodhyathaambudhee
Selecting a little from the fathomless ocean of *Mathanga Saasthra*
Told by the sage Palakapya to Romapada
I am presenting *Mathangaleela* for the scholars
To check and recognise if worthy.
(Trans. Poornima G.)

Neelakandan Mooss wrote about *Mathangaleela* thus. (We do not have any more information about the great poet. "*nrisimhayaadavow deithyasamooho graadaviidavow raaja maanowbhajee raajaraajamangala vaasinow*" [trans. I salute both Nrisimha and Yadava, who are wildfire to the forest of demons and also are shining at Rajarajamangala"] thus self-introduces the author. I have heard that this poet laureate has authored other works as well. It is said that the same poet has authored a book on cracker-production and its methods, titled, *Kambakkettu*, which is written in pure Malayalam.)

I remembered the third shlokam of "Dwidiyasargam" in *Mathangaleela* when I was beginning this narrative on the regal elephant, Kirangaattu Kesavan. The qualities of an elephant that Thirumangalath Neelakandan laid down in *Mathangaleela* applies to Kirangaattu Kesavan. I have heard that the round thick trunk in its resting position measures to three and a half circles. This has surprised many people. People who have seen him have experienced it. An elegant Kshathriyan, King of Elephants, attributes to his kingliness. A king has the right to kill. If a king kills, there is no punishment.

If the justice machinery orders to kill, killing is also justice. That's all I have to say about Kirangaattu Kesavan. In short, he is not a murderer. But he has killed his mahouts. We should think. Calling an elephant a murderer is human justice. It becomes a big crime when an elephant quarrels once or twice. But the elephant, a forest dweller, is brought to the human civilization, tortured and tamed, showcased in temple festivals and subjected to hard work to please humans. In the ensuing confusion, if a human gets killed, the elephant turns out to be the murderer. Humans will then punish him. Chaining the front and the hind legs together, piercing spears to the knees of the elephant! In the justice system of elephants, humans would be criminals. Do humans who preach human-rights think about elephant-rights? If they think human-life is more important than an elephant's-well, maybe!! My answer is, "I don't know."

Kirangaattu Kesavan, whose Kshatriya bravery brims from the tip of the tail to the trunk, feared only Mullan Sankaran, his mahout. There are stories that in merely the time taken for consecutive three lightning strikes, Kesavan walked to Kirangaattu Illam in Kochi from Malabar. That's the power of the mahout. It is all about training. Kesavan was also submissive to a Namboothiri in Poozhichooru[28]. That was love. He was a priest in the Kirangaattu Illam. Ganapathi-fire-ritual (Ganapathi *homam*), floral tributes (*pushpanjali*), prayer offerings in the Illam. By offering jaggery, slices of coconut and sweet porridge, the Namboothiri wrested Kesavan's love–a love-bond. Anytime the Namboothiri could go near the elephant. Even when he stabbed a mahout and the blood dripped from the tusk, Poozhichoor could go near him. When he says "come" and walks in front of the elephant, Kesavan would follow him like a puppy. Who said elephants do not have brains! Elephants display intellect, love, fondness, anger, anxiety and all such feelings. Humans do not have the brains to identify those.

---

28. The name of an illam.

There was another priest named Kurushaloor in Kirangaattu. He was a priest in the temple just outside the house. He had a rapport with all the other elephants in the house except Kesavan. Kesavan was the King. If a hundred people say, he will not listen! What a liking!! He likes one person. He will listen to him, that's it!!

Kesavan died on the 3rd or 4th of the Malayalam month of *Dhanu*[29] in Kollavarsham 1113[30]. He was bought from the Southern part of Kerala. He would have been bought from the Artist Pootti. Maybe from Kilimanoor Koyippandaala who bought Kesavan from Pootti. (There should be documents to prove these assumptions. However, like today, we didn't have legal documents and affidavits then. One's word was the only document.) For more than 20 years, Kesavan lived in Kirangaattu. His death was untimely when he was only 43.

The warrior-stories entangled with the history of Kesavan have attained a legendary status. It is an exaggeration that he has killed 25 people. The people in Kirangaattu say that he killed five. Along with Kesavan, another elephant was also bought and brought to the North of Kerala, by Thirunaavaaya Vaadhyaar. That was the time. Kings and the rich would buy elephants. Sometimes wood-sellers also buy. They do not need big elephants, though. They would need elephants that could lift huge logs of wood. There were elephants that have not seen festivals and have not been decorated for such events. Only elephants were employed for lifting logs in wood factories. That was a time when there were no machineries of today. The landlords send their elephants for such jobs when there were no festivals. The expenses of the elephant could be met this way.

The mahout of Kirangaattu Kesavan was famous as well– Sankaran Nair, aka, Mullan Sankaran. During that time,

29. Sagittarius sign of the Zodiac.

30. Malayalam era begins in 825 AD.

Malabar was under the British rule. So, the place was also called British Malabar. The entire Malabar had only one Collector. Ponnani-Chavakkad to Mangalapuram was one single district. The Collector was the supreme authority. Kesavan unchained himself in Malabar. Two to three days passed. No one could chain Kesavan. To avoid losses, the Collector commanded to shoot him. In 24 hours, if the elephant was unable to be chained he would be shot. This shoot is not to tranquilize; it is original. Those white bullets[31] and rifles. It will dig into Kesavan's body. "What can be done to avoid this situation," Thampurakkanmaar[32] thought. Finally, Sankaran was called. They told him what to be done.

"Yes, as you wish," Sankaran said.

"I can save him from the white man's gun-shot. But not sure if we can chain him. He is not letting anyone closer."

"Then, what can we do?" Thampuran shouted.

"The command is from the British Malabar. I shall bring him to Kochi. Then ... you know what to do." – Said Sankaran

"Enough! What Sankaran said is right. That's logic. If he is brought to our place, the British command does not apply. We can buy time until a new command is signed and passed."

"Good, Sankaran, you are brilliant. Then, don't waste time. The elephant is near Ponnani." Thampurakkanmaar commanded.

Sankaran Nair started his journey in a single oxen-driven bullock cart. Before evening, he reached near the elephant. Aiming at his ear, he went close to the angry elephant. He threw a stone on the elephant. Terribly shocked, he turned back. In a split of a second he threw another one, at the elephant's *thavalakkuzhi*[33]. He began dragging his forelimbs.

---

31. Referring to the British machinery
32. Plural form of Thampuran.
33. The depression behind the forelegs of the elephant, above the base of the foot.

Then went the long pole which thrust on his body. That was a loud scream. He peed and pooped. Screaming in pain, he ran without turning back and the Nair behind him. After passing Changaramkulam, Kesavan stopped. He was exhausted! Soon came the next throw with a sharp pointed spear. This lap, he reached Perumbilaavu.

"Great! He reached Madakshi Theesan's land. Let me try some tactics to chain him. They won't shoot now." "Hey Sankaran, come here … take this!"

The Thampurakkanmaar offered Sankaran dresses and money. That's the story. We do not need to measure the exaggeration and truth in this story. Through hearsay, elephant stories become popular. Told and retold, it heightens. As you measure, it goes low, that's the age old wisdom.

Most of the mahouts will tremble seeing the King of Elephants. That's when a boy belonging to the Nambiar caste who was not even 16 years old, came over. He hid himself in front of the outhouse. The eldest Thampuran asked "Um, what?"

"I am a Nambiar from the North. People told me you need a mahout."

"Okay, who are you? … Mahout's son?"

"No, I can unchain the elephant, where's he?"

Thampuran grew curious. "He is not even as tall as that log. Would he be mad or ….?" Thampuran thought.

"The elephant is tied outside, within the compound. He has begun his musth."

"Eesh … no problem …"

By cautioning him not to go too close to the elephant, the Thampuran asked the boy to see him and get back. He was sent to the plantation along with the servants.

After a while, the people in the Kirangaattu Mana got shocked hearing the trumpet of the elephant. No one has heard Kesavan roaring this way. The elephant used to silently bear Mullan Sankaran's long-pole trick!! The growling could be heard repeatedly, like thunder. There comes the boy with the long and short poles safely kept underarm. The shrunken Kesavan with shivering legs, walking behind the boy. Like the bulls pulling the cart which shits and pees several times, the elephant defecating on its way. Thampurakkanmaar saw this sight. The boy was asked to chain the elephant on to a mango tree, away from the house. Called the boy closer, gave him enough food, a dhothi and 100 rupees.

"Excellent, Nambiar, Excellent. Who taught you mahout-ship?"

"My mom!" He said, humbly.

"Shiva Shiva!! Heard what you said!."

"Very happy."

"But tell your mother, there is no elephant here for you to take care of!!"

The entire family stood staring at the Nambiar boy who kept the dhothi underarm and walked away.

This is also an elephant story. It proves the strength and mastery of a mahout.

Kirangaattu Kesavan was about 4 kol[34] tall. He was bought by a sage Namboothiri in Kirangaattu.

For many years, after Kesavan died, Kirangaattu Illam did not have elephants. Again, much later, elephant/elephants were bought and sold in Kirangaattu.

---

34. 4 *kol*, 4 finger = 9.5 feet.

Chapter 4

Poomulli Sekaran

Chambaapuriyilangeeshan roomapaadan prathaapavaan
Paalakaapyanoodiimattil kaykooppichodyamoothinaan
Sapthadhaathuthbhavavidham samgrahathil paranjupool
Munee madaavasthayinga, lenikkeerunnu samsayam
Dhaathuveethaashrayichittu, maadyathingal pravruthamaam
Randaamatheethileenmattil moonnaamdhaathuvilum munee!
Naalaamatheeyumanjum thaa, naarumeezhaamathullathum
Ithileethinebaadhichu pravarthikkum mahaamunee!
(*Hasthyayurveeda*, Palakaapyam, Chapter 31, Interpretation of Ashtavaydyan Vaidyamadham Cheriya Narayanan Namboothiri – "Madaavastha")

Romapada, the king of Angadesa,
Folding his hands
Asked sage Palakapya humbly, in Champapuri.
"Oh sage, you have narrated, in short, about
The seven stages of musth caused by seven minerals (7 dhatus)
Now doubts arise in me; depending on which mineral
The first stage starts.
Also, the second, the third, the fourth, the fifth, the sixth and the seventh
Work on the account of which of these minerals.

(Trans. Poornima G.)

Porayanoor Namboothiri bought three elephants from the Vaniyamkulam market sometime between 1870 and 1871 AD. He looked after them for about 20 years. He sold onc of them to Poomulli Namboothiri as the elephant was mischievous. He is Poomulli Sekaran. Sekaran lived a graceful life in Poomulli for over three decades. There were other elephants named Gopalan, Krishnankutty and Ramachandran in Poomulli. Ramachandran was bought from the Pathans[35] of Mysore for 1000-1500 *paras*[36]. Those days, people who belonged to the Mysore Kingdom would walk 5-6 elephants to Malabar. They sell them in the market. Their next option is illams. One such elephant owner brought an elephant to Poomulli Mana. He had to return as they could not agree on the price. Knowing that they were going to Desamangalam Mana, the father Namboothiri called them back and settled the purchase. Not in terms of money but paddy grains, as in the style of V. K. N's *Sir Chaathu* (famous Malayala writer noted for his satirical style of writing). The elephant that the Pathan sold was called Poomulli Ramachandran. The Namboothiris of Porayanoor Illam bought Kesavan from the Pathans and later sold it to the Poomulli Illam. Bargaining disgracefully for an elephant is a bad omen.

"For all those who know elephantology, particularly people who buy and sell, if they have a mutual agreement that is beyond the buyers' and the sellers' imagination it is a good omen. It is a mediocre business if the opinions of the buyer, seller and the persons who know the science are the same. If all the three have different opinions, it is not auspicious to buy or sell an elephant. The commodity turns disgraceful."

According to the Appendix in *Mathangaleela*, discussing the price should be done after the above words are quoted. Then the reasons for the value quoted are to be explained.

This is not the concern now. I am talking about the elephants in Poomulli. The richest landlord in Kerala was the

35. Pathans are a Muslim community in Mysore.

36. *Para* is a local measurement unit; 1 *para* is equal to 8 kilograms.

Namboothiris in Poomulli. There are other landlords who had the same status as the Namboothiris in Desamangalam, Olappamanna, Varikkaaseeri families and so on. Kothara Illam, which is near Poomulli, is just in the front. Apart from the Kings, the Namboothiris were the buyers of elephants and of course a few rich Nair families like Paliyam and Kavalappara also owned elephants. Even people belonging to Ezhava castes had elephants. Whatever the case, the elephant owner should be rich. All these people are known to the Pathans of Mysore, though they were outsiders. Some Muslim chiefs who owned wood-mills and spice businesses in the mountains of Wayanad also bought elephants from the Pathans. They needed elephants for labour. There are no Arattupuzha-Thrissur Temple festivals in North Malabar and Wayanad! In Central Kerala, elephants are used for temple processions. Height, beauty, statures, complexion are all concerns to be considered. Elephants with 20 nails are rare to find. But nails cannot go less than 18. If 16, the elephants can only be used for Shiva temples. If the elephant is good-looking, the sellers take them to the Kochi Kingdom. That's where one can get a good price. Kochi kingdom may not mean Kochi alone; it could also be central Kerala, the land of temple festivals.

There could be a lot of stories about the rich landlords. Stories about receiving treasures. Snake and elephant would manifest as luck-bringing child, male saviour and fortune-bringing goddess. There is a popular story of an elephant who went back to the forest and brought back a sack of gold to the illam. The king of snakes appeared and offered the famous "snake-ruby" *(nagamanikyam)*. Such sweet stories are passed on from generation to generation. There is a story about Poomulli Mana as well. (Though the members of the family do not believe in it, people outside believe that it is true, even now. They reason, "would anyone reveal if they have received a treasure?")

Even if people forget their fame about richness and elephants, Poomulli Mana will not be forgotten. The 6th

Thampuran (the head of the family in the 6th generation), who lived in the house was a Pandit, the lord of knowledge. *Hasthyayurveda* was popularised in Kerala by the Poomulli Mana. The reason for the work to be translated to Malayalam was the 6th Thampuran. It was translated by Narayanan Namboothiri from Vaidya Matamillathil; it was published by Mathrubhumi in 2006; it was read and seen only by Pandits in Kerala, the knowledgeable elephant-doctors until it was published for wider circulation in 2006. The translation was a blessing of the Palakappiya Maharshi. The treatise was equally useful to the traditional ayurvedic gurus and practitioners and also the modern doctors. The treatise will turn out to be a treasure even for the next generation as it has become popular now.

The Maharshi has stated that a king who does not possess an elephant is not a king.

"If one does not like a woman, he is not a man. If one does not like an elephant, he is not a king." (*Hasthyayurveda*—The translation of Vaidyanadan—Page 75).

Even if one is not a king, if one owns an elephant, one becomes a king. Elephant is a graceful creature. That's what's important.

This is Kaliyuga[37]. In Kaliyuga one can only see crossbreeds and complex caste of elephants. Pure breed *(Shudhabhadra)*, slow breed *(Manda)* and animal breed *(Mruga)* do not happen in Kaliyuga. This is not merely the story of elephants. All animals and pulses have become crossbreeds today. In this context, one need not think "why only elephants are crossbreeds?"

Whatever the type, musth is natural to elephants. During the spring season elephants in the forest will produce musth. This could also happen during other seasons, but in less intensity. It is in the monsoon season that the domesticated elephants

37. The fourth age of the world according to Hindu mythology—an age of total destruction.

show signs of musth. Local elephant-doctors know how to stop the process. Musth is believed to be created by the Brahman and attached to the body of elephants. As the responsibility of creation is entrusted with Brahman, every living organisms, land and symbolic beings have the image of the Naanmukhan.[38] Creation is according to the *Vedas*, that's important. "In the battle of Devasuran, the eight elephants (Ashtagajangal) who were the vehicles of the eight deities (Indradikalakar) ruling over the eight quarters of the Universe, ran with fear, to Brahman for refuge. Knowing the reason for their fear[39], created musth-man and possessed him into the elephants." — *Mathangaleela*. Madapurushashrishti, Shlokam 24, Translation by Cheruvalli Narayanan Namboothiri).

There is a detailed Chapter on musth of elephants in *Mathangaleela*. New Chapter. The chapter which contains 23 shlokams is titled "Treatments for curing Musth." They are:

1. *Gajasanthushti* (Joy of the elephant)
2. *Dhaatu vrudhi* (Swelling of the testicles)
3. *Dhaatu Saamyatha* (Comparison of the testicles)
4. *Madaheethu* (Causes of ejaculation)
5. *Mada sravasthaanangal* (Places of musth exudation)
6. *Ashtamadagunangal* (The eight qualities of semen)
7. *Madaniksheepanam* (Ejaculation of semen)
8. *Madavridhigunam* (Qualities of semen)
9. *Madabhalam* (The result of ejaculation)
10. *Madapthi lakshanam* (Characteristics of the flow of semen)
11. *Madakaalacheeshtakal* (Gestures during ejaculation)
12. *Madagajaprakruthi* (Nature of elephants during ejaculation)
13. *Madabaalyalakshanam* (External characteristics of semen)

---

38. The four-faced god; another name for Brahman.

39. They are Indra, Yama, Varunya, Kubera, Agni, Nigti, Vayu and Isana.

14. *Madaakshamathvam* (Intolerance during ejaculation)
15. *Gandhaavastha* (The status of smell)
16. *Madukrodhathwam* (Fury during ejaculation)
17. *Athimada lakshanam*
    (Characteristics of excessive ejaculation)
18. *Madanivrithi* (Remedies for illness during heat-period)
19. *Madaanandara bhalam (Characteristics after ejaculation)*
20. *Pradhamadwitheeya masa chikithsa*
    (The first two months of treatment)
21. *Thritheeya masa Chikithsa* (Three months of treatment)
22. *Madakopachikithsa* (Treatment for increase of semen)
23. *Vasheekaranaaushadham* (Medicines for seduction).

I can definitely say that if one learns *Mathangaleela* written by Thirumangalathu Neelakandan Mooss, all mischiefs of the elephants that one sees and hears will cease to exist. The reasons for elephant mischiefs are the elephants themselves. Human judgement would vouch that humans do not play any part in this. Elephants get angry when they are not given sufficient food and water, when they do not have enough sleep and when they are brutally tortured. They long for being unchained. We don't allow that; and all accusations are on the animal. Humans are offence-free. What love of animal, nature for those who think that the universe is created only for humans' comfort?

Most of the time, elephants that break the chains in anger stop when they see water. This is to quench their thirst, to dip and bathe. If we allow that, the elephant will obey. This freedom is not given to the elephant. They say they take "care" of the elephant. For instance, elephants are never allowed to walk but carried in vehicles. Do elephant-lovers know that elephants would love walking for 30 *naazhikas* (1 naazhika is about 1 mile) rather than standing while travelling in a truck for hours? In the forest, they walk for 30-50 *naazhikas* in search of food. If they don't walk enough, it will adversely affect their metabolism. Beatings on the tummy area of the elephants causes gastritis. The modern elephant-lovers think that elephants are a source to make money. Beating, thrashing and knife methods are all done after blocking their vision and chaining their legs. Hereafter, there will not be any elephant which would die naturally of old age.

Listen to the words of Acharya:

Naagaanaam vanavaasa eevavihitha-

Sthasyaapyalaabhaadasaa-

Thmyaakaamaashanapaanathashchavishamaa-

Jiirnaadibhirbhojanaiha

Ddhusthaaneeshwadanaadibhishchashayanaa-

Ddhooshaha samiiraadikaha

Kupyandhyaashushariiramaanasabhavaa-

Droogaamcha kurvandhi cha.[40]

(*Mathangaleela*, Ekaadashadhikaran, Gajarakshadevichaaram, Shlokam 43)

Elephants will be comfortable in the forest. When they are denied this opportunity but have to eat and drink what they dislike, they may get gastric diseases caused due to the other foods that they eat that cause indigestion. Travelling in unfavourable conditions causes sleeplessness, their physiological functions mediated by three humours–according to *Ayurveda* (*Vatham, Pitham* and *Kabham*)–change the constitution of their body. The imbalance of *vatham-pitham-kabham* in the body can cause various diseases, physically and mentally.

40. Translation in prose is given below.

Chapter 5

Nagaradhyakshan

(The Chief of Elephants)

Naagaadhyakshasthudhiimaannarapathisadrushoo-
Dhaarmikaaha swaamibhakthaaha
Shudhassathyaprathijnjoovyasanavirahitha-
Samyathaaksho vineethaha
Uthsaahiidrushtaakarma priyavachanarathaha
Sadgurooraathashaasthroo-
Dakshoo dhiirassharanyoogadaharanachanoo
Nirbhayassarvaveeththaa.
(*Mathangaleela,* Dwadashaadhikaram, Shlokam 1)

The master of elephant should be intelligent,
king-like, righteous and loyal
He should be pure-hearted, truthful,
devoid of seven blemishes (*Sapta Vyasanas*[41]),
foresighted and humble
Enthusiastic, acting wisely
according to the situations, dearly speaking
and well-taught in Shastras from a proper mentor (Guru)
Expert in all fields, brave, helpful and
approachable for others, efficient
in curing ailments and a person with vast knowledge.
(Trans. Poornima G.)

---

41. Drunkenness, womanizing, gambling, hunting, verbal harshness, harshness in punishments, wrongly spending money.

Prof. Sujatha, famous poet, after hearing the qualities of a mahout wrote: "Not one quality is possessed by the politicians who rule the people." One of those qualities is Vedic purity. When a topic is discussed, whatever it may be, it is presented without any loopholes. If one subject is studied in depth, the rest will naturally follow. That's why they say, a good word can change the world—the word will turn out to be the Kamadhenu[42] (goddess of cow) in heaven.

Even if all these qualities can't be seen in a person, there were people with immense experience and knowledge in one or two. Kadalayi Namboothiri was one such person. This story happened when he was too old to stand up on his own. In an elephant race in Pidikkapparambil, a huge elephant turned reckless. He had killed about 20 people earlier. Those days there were no intoxicating gun shots. Not knowing what to do, the elders and officials of the temple met Kadalayi Namboothiri. He said, "take me, along with this bed, to the ground where the elephant is, I will take care of the rest."

"No, no, in this condition ... not even able to stand up... no, do not engage in this adventure" – exclaimed the villagers unanimously.

Namboothiri said thus:

"Don't worry! Even earlier, I wasn't stronger than elephants."

That's a mahout. A stone. A stick. Anything is enough. Those days are gone. Today's methods are terribly cruel. By cutting a vein in the leg, giving electric shock and by 20 people who stand in a circle to beat the elephant down. Make the elephant unable to stand up by itself. Torture! Terrible torture! Beat until the front and hind legs injure, beat to break the eyes.

42. Kamadhenu is a miraculous cow that can give anything that its owner desires.

There are many elephants in this place whose front and hind legs are injured and eyes broken due to torturous beating. They are half-dead Ganapathis[43]. Yes, elephants are Ganapathis to us. *Ganapathayee namaha*[44] (A humble salutation to Lord Ganesha).

The story of Kadalayi Namboothiri is an old one. Paroli lived in the recent times. Paroli is the name of his illam. He had the freedom to call the king by his name. When EMS[45] became the chief minister, he went to see Paroli "Kunju." Paroli is bold enough to call the king of Kollamkodu, Sir Vasudevaraja, by the name Vengunaadu elder Nambidi[46]. He goes to Desamangalam, Avanapparambu, Kirangaattu, every day. He is dark complexioned, with a pot belly, long hands and legs; he has long hair which is tied behind, decorated with lily flowers, that any woman would envy; he wears a red bindi; his mouth is red with chewing betel leaves and has holy ash-lines on his dark hands. His mouth is full of the juice of betel leaves and rude words. He travels on a single bullock cart. The elephant behind. There would be vegetables, coconut oil, hand-scraper and rice in the cart. The fat, pot-bellied man would reach on top of the elephant swiftly if needed. After Kadalayi Namboothiri, Paroli was the greatest mahout that Kerala has ever seen.

He has scientifically learned elephantology, face to face from a guru, and yet he is known as a trickster. The *avatar* of the "casket and ball" games in magic. A Vazhakkunnam[47],

---

43. Here, a satirical consideration of all elephants as Lord Ganesha.
44. This salutation is more a sarcastic one
45. EMS Namboothiripad was the first chief minister of Kerala as it was formed as a state in 1956.
46. A casual way of calling the name (a shortened form of Namboothiri, meaning Brahmin).
47. Vazhakkunnam is a famous magician in Kerala.
48. The art of taming elephants.

in reality. He, the king of magic and hypnotism, learned Anappaavu[48] staying at the Kodungalloor Gurukulam. He also learned the techniques of thootti (hook), kuntham (spear) and cherukole (short pole). Not only had he learnt how to sit on the elephant and the techniques with legs *(kaal kodukkal)* but also the body-flexibility to tame while sitting on the elephant. He became an expert in magic and the technique of putting elephants to sleep (*Mohanidra Vidya*). Only when someone asked him, he imparted this knowledge. One should know the following when using the hook:

"*Eeshathsparshana, piidanaa, thihananaa-*

Nyuthkshipyasampiidana"

(one should touch the elephant with the hook for torturing in specific ways)

The unique techniques of the hook that he knew died with him. The only resort was to shoot the elephant to intoxication. They shot over 500 bullets into the heads of elephants.

Cheettunni Narayanan Nayar was only four and half feet in height. He looked like a midrib of a coconut leaf, pierced into a baby coconut. He has a usual stomach ache. His food is baking soda and yellow fiery chillies. He stoops, sits down to massage his belly. He looks like a stick as thin as the little finger. He gets on top of any elephant like a squirrel. Like flipping the *dosa* for the other side to cook, he would make the elephant lie down on the left to the right side. Chettunni was well-liked by the eldest Namboothiri, Avanapparambu Achan Thampuran. He has bought and sold many elephants. But if you ask him, whether he is a mahout, he would just think and not answer.

There were a lot of dependents of the Avanapparambu Illam who later became mahouts. Well known among them is Velutheedan Goyinnan. A tall man with strong muscles. Very healthy. If he aims and throws a stone at any coconut tree, a coconut will fall. The stone will produce a murmuring sound while flying. He has taken care of many elephants. Witty and fearless! Once in Desamangalam Illam, a mahout tied the elephant and left the place. Goyinnan was asked to untie the elephant and bring him to the illam. Goyinnan went near the elephant, saw him and returned.

"What?" Thampuran asked, hinting why he did not bring the elephant.

"Master, I cannot do that!" Goyinnan replied.

"What, did you say, you can't?" Thampuran asked.

"Yes master, to unchain him, you only need to send one of your servants. I need not go to unchain the elephant whose front and hind legs are tied together. Ask me to bring a mischievous elephant who can't be tied. I will do as you say."

"Oh wow! Give him two dhotis." All the thampurakkanmar liked his courage.

That was Velutheedan Goyinnan. He will fight face to face. Not allowing any legs to touch the ground he will make the elephant dance. He just needs the long pole and a stone. But he never harms the elephant like it is done today. The sensitive areas of the heart and the penis would not be touched, as such harm could affect the lifespan of the elephant. But he inflicts pain. Knives, bull-hooks, whips and metal pipes were not used then. The owners loved their elephants. Elephants were not objects to make money. An elephant was a prestige to the family.

There are two unique mahouts, I will introduce now. Both of them belonged to the Nambiar caste in Changazhikodu. Chengazhi Yashmans[49] were the leaders of Samuthiri's (landlord) Aranoottuvar. They wore the sacred thread *(puunuul)*. Somehow an uncle and nephew became mahouts. With white sacred thread. A lot of hair knotted to the forehead *(Kuduma)*. White

49. Yashmans (in print Malayalam register, Yajamaan) were landlords.

shirt and dhoti. Typical Yashmans. The uncle was a sorcerer. A sorcerer who went to the mount of Pazhani in penance, a 101 times. He danced as if his legs are stuck with thorns. His nephew sells curd and butter. Those days if one needs a pot of curd, one should depend on the Nambiar. Seldom though, if the landlord-families craved for sugar-porridge, they depended on the Yashman/Nambiar. One has to milk 50 cows to collect 2 *paras*[50] of milk. There are no cows in the place that give more than 3 *naazhis*[51]. Both these Yashmans became mahouts. Even then, they had food only from illams and temples. They are the heirs of Veerasenan, who during the battle, on his deathbed, bit his own hand to quench his thirst with his blood because he refused to drink the water offered by the Shoodran[52].

Another community was Muslims. It is not common to see Muslim mahouts. For Hindu festivals, non-Hindus are not allowed. Yet, there was one Muslim mahout in the place. He wore a thick green belt, a knife on it and had a moustache. A very innocent Muslim. A saintly man who left his job in the rock quarry and became a mahout. They say, "the elephant that was touched by a Pathan." Yet, he took elephants to Hindu festivals. For some time, a Tamil Brahmin also was seen with him as a mahout.

Mahoutship is a paid job now. For every procession, they are paid Rs. 1000-1500. This is for their expenses. Salary is a different payment. They also get gifts. If the elephant carries the deity, the payment is more.

In short, mahoutship is not a bad job. It is also not death food[53]. Not as dangerous as lorry and bus drivers. You also need not walk. Nowadays, all elephants are transported in

50. 1 *para* is about 8 kilograms.

51. 4 *naazhi* = 1 *idangazhi*; 10 *idangazhi* = 1 *para*.

52. The lowest of the caste system.

53. Meaning, earnings for livelihood that might kill the mahout.

large vehicles. Elephant-vehicles will go to the festival ground. Then to another one.

Mathangaleela says that the hook should be used only on the following body parts:

1. Adornment
2. The vessel-shaped part on the forehead of the elephant, which is called *vidu*
3. Neck
4. The corner of the outer eye called *niryaanam*
5. Head
6. The part below *vidu* called *avagraham*

   (*Mathangaleela*, Angushaprayogam)

Chapter 6

Pidikal

(She - Elephants)

She-elephants are described thus:

Elephants that are "Six *muzham*[54] tall, eight *muzham* in length and nine *muzham* in breadth are the best. Five *muzham* tall, seven *muzham* length, eight *muzham* breadth are the mediocre ones. Four *muzham* tall, six *muzham* length and seven *muzham* breadth are the base ones. There is a way to measure the elephant—from the eyes to the tip of the tail, from the nail to the place where the elephant sits. Height—from the chest. This is the rule of measurement. If the measurements are not done this way, it is inauspicious. If done this way, it is auspicious."

(*Mathangaleela*. From the 1942 version published by Bhaashavyakhanasahitam, University of Travancore; Appendix 3, Bhashagadhyaroopam [The structure of Prose Language])

All the women, women-empowerment groups, women writers, kindly pardon me for saying a truth. The male race of all species is more beautiful than the female—from elephant to goat, eagle to mosquito, and peacock to hen!

54. 1 *muzham* is 46.66 centimetres.

Isn't that true? Yes. There is a reason for this. The female should increase the race. So, they should go in search of the males. Men do not go in search of women. Women will run after men. When the peacock dances with its spread-out feathers, peahens will circle it and dance with him. The bull-elephant's secretion of the musth odour and the nod of his head while he quakes the earth will attract a few she-elephants. These are all the characteristics of animals. But the value that humans give to bull-elephants, they don't give to she-elephants.

Mathangaleela instructs:

Elephants that are one-eyed, single-tusked, lamed, and deaf will get only half the price. Elephants that have broken tails *(munduvaalan)* and torn ears *(chevimuriyan)* will get only 1/3rd of the price. Bull-elephants with no tusks *(moozha)* get only 1/4th of the price. She-elephants get only 1/3rd. If the elephants have disfigured tusks (ugly elephants [*thiikkomban*][55], thin [*chillikkomban*] and small [*unnikkomban*] tusks; elephants with one of the tusks sticking up) only 1/8th. This is the norm for bargaining and selecting elephants. (The aforementioned terms for disfigured tusks maybe interpreted contextually, like, a tusk with a hole in it might also be considered disfigured).

You know that this norm is not applicable to every animal. More expensive are the cows and she-goats. Bulls and he-goats end up in slaughterhouses. Then comes the rooster.

Even the circus people seldom use she-elephants. So is the case with bull-elephants without tusks. However, she-elephants or bull-elephants without tusks *(moozha)* are best for cycling and somersaulting in the circus. Neelakandan Mooss in his *Mathangaleela* has not mentioned many things

55. Any ungraceful elephants could be grouped in this category.

about bull-elephants without tusks. The word, *moozha*, does not appear in the dictionary as well. But she-elephants are discussed. *Moozha* is not hermaphrodite, but bull-elephants without tusks. However, they are fertile.

African she-elephants have tusks. That shouldn't have been. Those who have seen great Indian bull-elephants would think that the she-elephants with tusks are disgraceful and obscene. Maybe we are not used to seeing the African she-elephants with tusks.

Lottery 1 Rupee
First Prize
an ELEPHANT

Chapter 7

Shodathy

(The Raffle)

Hiinaadhikyanakhaamgadrushyavrushanoo
Hraswaamgulirvaamanoo
Mandhukoodarakubjaniilashabala-
Shyaamaabhathaalusthadhaa
Sthuulashchaathithanuurjalookasadrushaaha
Shwaathulyapaarshwadwayoo
Ruuksha nirmadaniichapushkarakaraha
Puujyoona chaayamgajaha

(*Maathangaleela*, Thritheeyadhikaaram[56]; Inauspicious qualities, Apoojyagajam Shlokam 1; Ardhadeviyakhyaa-nam—Cheruvalli Narayanan Namboothiri)

Elephants with disproportionate body organs - long or short,
Testicles exposed, small fingers, and short (dwarf)
Flat stomach like that of a frog, bent body,
palate dark blue or multi-coloured
Body too fat or too lean, leech-like
appearance of the two (lateral) sides
Resembling that of a dog
Rough body without musth fluid, dry trunk;
are not ideal and beneficial.

(Trans. Poornima G.)

56. Third Chapter.

When one says that the elephants are useless, one needs to think, useless for who, why, what. Usually "usefulness/uselessness" is decided with respect to the owner of the elephant. Would the elephant bring grace to the owner? Or is he going to be doomed? There are elephants that will bring grace to the owner and disgrace to the mahout. It is good for the person (mahout) who takes care of the elephant and otherwise it could be bad for the elephant and the owner. This also could happen. According to the aforementioned characteristics, it is said that such elephants are useless. It does not say that the elephant is bad.

A very mischievous elephant can turn out to be graceful, later. It is also possible that a calm elephant can doom a family. Modern science will not accept that these are rational. The raw can either fruit or become dry and wither, plantains do not get to ripe if some people cut them off the plant. They will dry and shrink. If some of them milk a cow that gives much milk, it will stop mulching. "Pulikkaranam" [57] is a Malayalam saying. These are all qualities of the blood. There are some people who argue for this. These are all traditional knowledge acquired through hearsay and experience.

Shodathy! Shodathy means raising money by selling tickets and randomly selecting a winner. This money that he/she receives is lottery. This lottery was administered by the Namboothiri family of Avanapparambu. The Namboothiris at Avanapparambu were lords-lords of the king that rules the place. When the king visited the mana, they decorated the steps to the storeroom of the house with *paras* [58] made of gold. But the king did not like this kind of rich display of their lordship.

57. Literally, tiger handed. This dictum means that if a person who possesses the qualities of a tiger touches a cow, it will touch only for the "wrong" reasons.

58. Vessel for measurement.

His heart pained. The hearsay is that a large amount of their wealth was confiscated by the King. The family practiced elephant treatment, and treatments for poisoning. The great grandfather of the recent poison-doctor and elephantology scholar Maheswaran Avanapparambu, had bought and sold several elephants. There were no Namboothiris who bought and sold elephants during that time. Not only Namboothiris, none other. They had stopped the market which sold elephants. It is recently that Thirukkangottu Narayana Pattar opened the route to the Patna-Mysore market. An elephant route like the ancient silk route. The lottery was not organised by the Avanapparambu family. Some humourists have made a story out of this. Though bad, the story is enjoyable.

This lottery elephant's name was Kuttykrishnan. A good labourer-elephant. Does not like processions. That may be the reason why he wouldn't be sold. The Avanapparambu[59] had decided to sell the elephant. So, he played a trick. He started a lucky draw. Draw arranged for Onam. The first prize is a tusker. The price of the ticket is rupee one. We don't know if anyone else would had purchased tickets. Anyway, a betel leaf merchant bought a ticket. After Onam, the merchant was brought to the Illam for the prize–the elephant–to be delivered. The elder in the Avanaparambu family would have thought in his mind that he got rid of that disgraceful elephant.

The mahout of the elephant walked the elephant to the new owner's house and tied him there. He then met the owner. "Master, I need a copper vessel to serve water to the elephant." The betel leaf merchant unfolded his chest in pride. "So, I have become the owner of an elephant." He tied the towel on his head, majestically. Went to the kitchen and brought the biggest

59. Referring to the great grandfather of Maheswaran.

copper vessel in the house. The mahout filled water in it. The elephant drank two handful of water and stamped the vessel. Pleeeeee. The copper vessel flattened. The wife of the seller kept her hands on her head, began crying. That was the only piece of copper vessel in the house.

One cannot give water to the elephant in a mud pot. Not knowing what to do, the owner was stupefied. That was the time when the mahout came.

"Sir, we are three. You must give two *naazhis*[60] to each person, so six *naazhis*. A little salt and chillies. We do not need any vegetables; we will pick them from the garden, instead. We will pluck some drumsticks, as well (Moringa)".

The betel leaf merchant, began calculating-three times a day, six *naazhis* of rice each. That is total of eighteen *naazhis*. Whatever, one *anna*[61] for groceries, oh my God!

Two days passed. On the third day, when the mahouts were walking the elephant to the river for bathing him, he shook the central pole that holds the roof of the house. That just came off, along with a few lines of tiles and other such poles. The mahout stopped the elephant. Gave him one. In the heat of the moment, "shodathy" turned and pushed the coconut tree by the side. It fell. The elephant stepped down to the paddy field. By the time the mahout chained the elephant; there appeared 4-5 accusers. "My entire field is damaged. 10-*paras* of rice-field was destroyed. 200 measures of rice!" "On his way he kicked my pregnant cow." One by one people came to claim their losses. They all got together for compensation. The tactical mahout, now, asked for his salary.

60. Two *naazhi* is roughly 500 grams.

61. 1 *anna* is 1/16th of a rupee.

What more to say! His wife left the house with his children. The betel leaf business stood still. The owner didn't know what to do.

At the end, with a stable mind, the betel leaf merchant, along with the mahouts and the elephant went to meet the Avanapparambu Thampuraan.

"Master, here is your elephant!" Kindly return my Rupee 1 for the elephant.

This is the story.

The Namboothiris joke that the word lottery was thus born.

During those days, exactly six years ago, there were no family in Thrippunithura and the entire Kerala who bought and sold so many elephants.

There was an elephant named Kunju in Avanapparambu. He was mischievous. Many elephants died due to Kunju's stabbing. They say that mahoutship is a dangerous profession. Well, which profession is not dangerous! If one is a driver, one may meet with an accident. Not only kill oneself, but the driver could also kill the others in the vehicle. Mahoutship is not that dangerous. It is a boastful job. The job is an embodiment of adventure. If one sees Guruvayoor Kesavan marching forward with his tusks held high—dear Guruvayoorappan, what a beauty! What a story!

Chapter 8

Chirackal Paramu

Prathyuhavyuuhavicheedakaarakangananaayakan
Jayippu sthirasambathaay gajabhakthanidarshakan
Aamoodanum pramoodan thaan sumukhan durmukhanthadhaa
Avikhnan vikhnaharthaavum heeramban gananaayakan
Lamboodaran gajamukhan dhuumakeethu gajaananan
Ellaathilum ganeeshante ee naamangal smarikkanam.

(Hasthyayurveda, written by Palakapya Maharshi begins thus. Translation: Ashtavadyan Vaidyamadham Cheriya Narayanan Namboothiri*)*

Lord Ganesha, the abolisher of arrays of hindrances
Symbol of devotion towards elephants; triumphs as eternal wealth.
He is indeed *aamoda, pramooda, sumukha and durmukha*
avighna, vighnahartha, heramba, gananaayaka
lambodara, gajamukha, dhuumaketu and gajaanana
All these synonyms of ganesha should be remembered on all occasions.

(Trans. Poornima G.)

Bharat is the land of Rishis. Those visionary poets had acquired all knowledge in the world. They learned the pure, lofty and excellent spiritual techniques to the lowly, vile and impure bloody techniques to create science. There was no truth that they did not experience. Truth is science. They learned Ayurveda, elephant-Ayurveda and tree-Ayurveda. They preached the entire world and everything in it to be peaceful and happy. We still enjoy the fruit of that good advice.

There are elephants even outside India. It is possible that African elephants belong to a more traditional race than the Indian ones. But a complete science on elephants was born only in India. The original *Elephantology* treatise has 171 Chapters and 12,000 shlokams in it-just to tell you the propensity of the work. It is recently that the veterinary science universities have introduced elephantology as an optional subject. Animal science that was born and developed outside India has done extensive research on horses, dogs and other domestic animals. Scholars produced and published scientific studies on them. Yet, I have not heard of such a study on elephants.

Internalising the body and soul of *Hasthyayurveda* written by Palakappiya Maharshi (in India), there were a few other works on elephants that were published. I am told that the book on elephantology published by Saraswathi Mahal Library, Thanjavoor, is an excellent work. *Mathangaleela* written by Thirumangalathu Neelakandan in Malayalam is a famous work. Elephantology works have been published in Assamese, as well. *Hastha Vidyarthava*. The translation of this work is available in English. *Gajarakshathantram*, written by Manikyamangalathu Sankaran Nambiar, in Malayalam is also a useful treatise. I also hear that there are works like *Aanapparu* written in Malayalam. Works from the ancient times dealing with the subject of the science of saving elephants and people who studied them carefully have immensely contributed to the area of elephantology. Long before veterinary surgeons were produced in India, local medical practitioners' (*Naattu Vaidyar*) services were the only availability. Even today, elephant owners depend on *Naattu Vaidyar* for treatments.

Like the elephants that are known for their height, beauty and sweet behaviour, there are elephants that are notorious for their mischiefs as well. There are elephants, when an opportunity arrives, maul humans to death, during heat or even without (mauling elephants and humans are a delight to some elephants). There is a temple called Chirackal near the place, Paavartty. There was an elephant named Paramu in the temple.

The Namboothiris in Maravancheri[62] take care of this boy-tusker. The main offering of the temple was liquor and fowl. The goddess had an angry presence. Even today the goddess is known for her awe. Paramu is the first elephant of the temple. A black guard of the first order. He was familiar with having liquor and chicken. Environmentalists might be interested in knowing how vegetarianism, Brahmin-animal relationships transformed this way. The context moulds the behaviour. Darwin and Marx, more or less, argue the same. They may or may not have, but Chirackal Paramu turned out to be a "non-vegetarian" and a murderer. In 1976, he died.

I don't know how many mahouts were exactly killed. Many murders are thrust on Chirackal Paramu. With so many murders and a bad name, he could be accused of doing anything. That is human behaviour. Towards his latter life he turned peaceful. Ten years earlier, he kicked a famous mahout named Kodiyan Achuthan. The mahout did not die. The elephant dabbed him as he stopped for urinating while walking the elephant. His three ribs broke. But he lived for several years after the incident.

There were three Achuthans. Nattathachuthan, Padickal Achuthan and Kodiyan Achuthan. The Achuthan-trio. The three of them were extreme idols. There are three other such idols—Chattootty Narayanan, Mulloor Sankaran, Velutheedan Goyinnan. In the chapter titled "Nagaradhyakshan" (The Chief

62. The name of an illam.

of Elephants), there is a brief description of mahouts. While referring to Chirackal Paramu, Kodiyan Achuthan cannot be forgotten.

The name of the goddess, Chirackal Bhagavati, is uttered by the villagers with fearful hesitation. The temple trusteeship was managed by a Nair family. The priestly affairs were managed by Parayar, a Dravidian caste. A traditional family. A temple with good income. The trustees always owned elephants. Some of them were majestic procession elephants. Yet, the family name Chirackal brought Paramu to the memory of people. Sometimes, thugs are more known in a place than saintly lords. Some of those thugs could even be honoured for the aura of some disguised greatness. Even then it is important to think about one thing. No elephant, no animal will go out of the forest to kill a human. There is a saying, "it is difficult for an elephant-mauled person to die and a snake-bitten person to live." If an elephant should kill someone, first, he should step into the trap-ditch to teach the elephant lessons, tamed and be brought immediately to the human society. When the elephant is here, he should be walked without any chains. Without any sense one should get closer to him physically. It is only then can an elephant attack. Phew!

How many obstacles should the elephant pass to be able to maul or kick someone? What about snakes, then? In this temple[63] of Parasuraman[64] we have snakes everywhere. No place without snakes. They creep around on the surface of

---

63. Refers to Kerala State

64. Parasuraman is believed to have created Kerala (then included parts of the present Karnataka and Kerala). Read the story of Parasuraman here: https://www.indiastudychannel.com/forum/25456-Story-birth-Kerala.aspx#:~:text=As%20per%20the%20Hindu%20mythology,half%20Kshatriya%20and%20Half%20Bramin.&text=Parasurama%20wants%20to%20stop%20it%20once%20for%20all.

the earth. They might be hidden in the heap of dry leaves and sand-hills. There could be snakes on the ways that humans trail. Even though snakes bite only a few number of people, it is quite easy to get bitten by snakes. That's why I said it is difficult for a person not to get bitten by a snake in this Kingdom[65] of snakes!!

Progressively, I should say that the Chirackal temple was an institution that strongly opposed the social order of the caste system. Not today's story. At least in Kerala, caste is not a big concern. Religion is the problem here. During those times when the caste problem did not have a resolution, an untouchable became the priest of a Nair temple. The most famous priests performed the rituals in Elavally Puliyannoor. The family that took care of the temple was Palliyana, a Nair family in Poorangattu. There are similar temples like these. Temples that belong to the Namboothiris but rituals performed by Nairs to the Ezhava-women gods. These are practices prevalent in the society which challenged the caste structure. They were all descendants of the Parayi who gave birth to 12 children.[66]

The caste of elephants in the four aeons (yugas) are of four types. In the Krithayugam, they belonged to the *Bhadrajaati* (caste), and they were the best. In the Threethaayugam, *Mandajaati* and in Dhwaparayugam they were *mrigajaati* (animal). In Kaliyugam, it is *Mrigasangeernajaati*. Every *jaati* is created compatibly, according to the *yugas*. Depending on the characteristics of the time/age, *mrigajaati* changes.

Prathyeekam bhadrajaathidiprokthalakshana sangarath
Sangeernajaathya mathangaha kalua thee bahulaayugee

65. Refers to Kerala State

66. A prevalent myth in Kerala about the unity of caste that all castes are born of a low-caste woman from the Paraya community.

The ideal characteristics of elephants are described in *Bhadrajaati*

When hybridized, becomes *Sangeernajaati* (a complex *jaati*)

In Kaliyuga, such elephants are plenty.

(*Mathangaleela*, Pradhamaadhikaaram, Shlokam 30. The interpretation of Cheruvalli Narayanan Namboothiri)

Chirackal Paramu was a hybrid with excellent elephant qualities. Darker complexion. Behavioural qualities, low. Kingly-qualities, a little bit. The fearsome Chirackal Bhagavati may have liked these qualities. Paramu belonged to the *Mrigajaati*. Astrologically, he must have been born in the Kali during the rainy season. It might be difficult to control his anger.

(Mrigalakshanam [Characteristics of Animal], *Mathangaleela*)

There is a saying in Malayalam: "One may trust a robber; but never a runt." Paramu was short and so couldn't be trusted.

Nowadays, foresters and elephant-doctors believe that there is yet another jaati of elephants–Kallana. It is a peculiar caste. Will not grow taller than 5 feet. The tail touches the ground; needle-trunks. It is not heard that such elephants are captured. I don't remember seeing anything about it in elephantology (Hasthyayurveda). It is not a dwarf. Scientifically they are called Mammoth. Chirackal Paramu did not belong to this caste. He was a common mountain-dweller. Brought prosperity to the owner. Is that not enough? Even now, the place Chirackal is synonymous with Chirackal Paramu.

Vajraardhachandranakhakeethaka kandakaabha-
Shchathwara eeva srunayoovihithaamuniindreeha

(*Mathangaleela,* Abgushabhedangal, Interpretation of Cheruvalli)

The sages had confirmed four kinds of goads:
Like *Vajraayudham*[67], crescent-like
Like fingernail
Like the thorns of pineapple plant.
Lord of goads, the *Ankushapurusha* resides on each of these
To control problematic elephants in musth.

(Trans. Poornima G.)

---

67. *Vajraayudham* is a weapon known for its swiftness and destructive power. In Hindu mythology, Lord Indra possesses it.

kavalappa
komban
one book was
11th lunar
inside
temple
the book
komban
poet
get it
there.
buy two
copies ? that will be the great

Chapter 9

Kavalappara Komban

(The Bull-Elephant of Kavalappara)

Chambaapuriyilangeeshan paalakaapyanoodingane
Aduthu vinayathoode choodichusaavakaashamaay
Yaathonnaanunmadanakamennathaanakku cholluka

(*Hasthyayurveda*, Kshudraroga sthaanam, Chapter 33, Interpretation of Vaidyamadham Cheriya Narayanan Namboothiri)

Romapada, the king of Angadesa, in Champapuri
Asked the sage Palakapya, slowly and humbly:
Which factor makes an elephant undergo musth?
(Trans. Poornima G.)

Lunacy is a disease that is commonly seen in elephants today. Humans are also commonly identified with lunacy. From lunacy to insanity, one loses control of the mind. They say it is in Kerala that there are many mentally ill people. For many things we score the first. Suicide, drinking, lunacy, molestation of women, divorce and now extremism—I suspect!

There was a tusker-character named Kavalappara Komban in literature—poetry and stories. All of that is not imaginary creation. A poor thing that only killed 18 people. It may be with no other option that the elephant was given to the Koodal Manickyam Temple. The story is that it has never killed anyone else after the elephant reached the temple. Medical practitioners say that no sleep or too much of sleep is lunacy. I am not saying that Kavalappara Komban was lunatic. Elephants that kill humans are usually mentally disturbed. Elephants are vegetarians. Lion, tiger, leopard are meatarians. They have to kill. Don't they have to kill to eat?

Wild elephants do not kill humans. If one gets in front of a mischievous elephant, the elephant may kick or stab to get rid of him/her. It is easy for wild animals to feed on the cultivation of humans in the wetlands of the mountains. Paddy, wheat and vegetables are very tasty dishes to these animals.

It is through song books that Kavalappara Komban became famous. A humourist had written a book titled *Kavalappara Komban*. It is a song that is self-published. His bad luck, not one copy of the book was sold. But that author was not dejected. On the 11th lunar day *(ekadasi)* of the Vedic calendar, he stood on the inside of the road to Guruvayoor. He stopped people who went into the temple and tactically requested. "Aren't you all going to the temple on an *ekadasi*? From there, you might want to buy the book titled *Kavalappara Komban* written by The Great Poet Panickar. Can you buy two copies for me as well? That will be a great help. There will be sellers on the road. They sell this book."

The great poet, Panickar (I do not know the real name of the author until I wrote this note). He made an understanding with people going to Guruvayoor-Nelluvaaya-Thiruvillamala on *ekadasi*. What more to say! *Kavalappara Komban* became famous. By that time, an agent sold about 10,000 copies of the book. We do not know if the businessman is The Great Poet, Panickar himself. The poet's trick and the book were successful. Any MBA holder would try this business tactic!

Major among the elephant-families[68] in Central Kerala are Desamangalam, Varikkasseri, and Olappamanna. Most of the landlords bought elephants. Seldom people who weren't landlords also bought elephants. There was no price for areca nut poles. And there were plenty of screw pine plants near the streams, both for the elephants to feed on. The only expense was the

68. Families who own elephants.

salary and food of the mahout. There are temple festivals and celebrations for it. Like these days, there were no festivals 365 days a year. Every day there are festivals now. No special days, festivals everywhere. Not only Hindus conducted festivals like *Kumbha/Sivarathri, Makarabharani*. Even Christians and Muslims use elephants for their festivals in processions. Offering to God is common among Muslims. That could be the reason why businessmen reared about 10-15 elephants. Whatever the price is, there are people to buy elephants. I know the story of two elephants—babies—being bought for Rs.3000 in 1953. Today, a good tusker costs about Rs.30 lakhs.

Elephant's vengeance and love are well known. Elephant's likes and dislikes are not only towards the owner and the mahout. It shows love towards domestic animals. It is common that in families that rear fowls, dogs are also nurtured. It is a practice that the owner does not kill one's own fowls. The dog knows that the fowls are also part of the family. Elephant is also like that. One could see cow-calves sleep near mischievous elephants. These are all common sights. Nature of animal life. No animal hurts an organism which would love them. Except humans, probably.

Many mahouts drink. Not today, then! Today liquor in Kerala is life-water, the *Kamadhenu* of the Government. Those days, foreign liquor-shops weren't there. In cities there could be. But common people cannot enter there. Arrack-shops were also very few. Toddy-shops were available, but only a few in number. Liquor was prohibited in Thalappilly Thaluk when this incident took place. But in the nearby Thrissur Taluk, one can drink. In the boundary of the Taluk there is a functional excise office. They levy excise duty there. Our mahout would have been drunk when bringing the elephant from Thrissur after the temple-festivals. He would also have stuck two bottles of arrack in his waist. When they come near the border in Thalappilly, the mahout would just sit on the ground with folded legs and tell the elephant, "Son, there are policemen there. I have bottles in my waist. They will confiscate the bottles. Take me and keep me on the ground, beyond the vicinity of the authorities."

Responding to the need of the mahout, the elephant will gather him in his trunk and keep him on the ground way beyond the excise office. Seeing this incident several times, it seems a resident humourist said, "you don't trouble the elephant this way. You take the four-feet detour through the paddy fields. Even if we see you and the elephant, we will pretend not to have seen you both."

There were such elephants. Today, as well. But they undergo cruel punishments!!

Elephants have hysteria and epilepsy. Both are different. Hysteria is possible. It is curable. Torture, punishment, sleeplessness, lack of enough food and water, bustle during temple festivals, body aches during travel (now in trucks) are the reasons for hysteria. Get rid of these reasons, the elephant will be cured.

From the age of the Vedas, elephants have been captured and trained for battles and festivals. Acharyan describes four important ways of capturing elephants in the 19th chapter of *Mathangaleela*. This is explained in the chapter titled "Gajagrahavichaaram" (Elephant Husbandry). They are:

1. *Anugatham*
2. *Paarshagarthaadikarnam*
3. *Aapaadam*
4. *Avapaadam*

Anugatham is a way in which the elephant is captured when he/she gets tired after a chase. The system called the Mysore Khedda[69] is a good example. Ropes that are 60 *kol*[70] in length and knotted and hid in about 1 *kol*-deep holes to trap the elephants. 10-12 knots. Dried leaves are covered below the holes. Soft mud is spread on top to hide the ropes. There is a way to bind the elephant with ropes after his/her legs gets trapped in the knot. Once the holes are readied, lotus, plantain tree and sugarcane are

69. Read about Mysore Khedda here: https://www.evolveback.com/kabini/mysore-khedda/

70. 1 *kol* is about 70 centimetres.

planted over it. The ends of the ropes are tied on the nearby trees. Experts and tricksters hide themselves behind the trees. Elephants that come for food gets trapped and can be captured this way. This is *Aapaadam*. *Avapaadam* is the elephant-ditch method.

Wild elephants are captured using trained elephants *(Thaappana)*. Mahouts hide in a net tied under the stomach of she-elephants. When the bull-elephants come getting attracted to the she-elephants, they are captured using ropes. What a treachery! Now, they can capture elephants using sedatives, rather than the elephant-ditch method. But elephant-capturing is prohibited. How good! Elephants are soon getting extinct. Particularly, the elephant-caste in Kerala.

There are stories of the greatness of musth elephants in battle fields. The chief commander and the warriors abandoned the king thinking that he died as he fell from the elephant, getting spear-stabbed by the enemy. They had to lead the battle, however. The enemies did not know that the King fell. If they knew, they would begin the winning celebrations. That's even more dangerous. The commander-in-chief led the battle. At the end, they won the battle. But the body of the king was missing. Where did the holy body disappear? When they turned back, they saw the elephant safe-guarding the king's body near a rock-hill. They noticed the blood-like fluids on the trunk of the elephant—Elephant's sweat that was. They said that the elephant was swaying his trunk to cool the body of the king.

There are many such surprising incidents. How many elephants did the great Sri Kottarathil Sankunni immortalize in *Aytheehyamala*. Those elephants attained a divine aureole than the Diggajangal.[71] Let us utter the synonyms of elephants like divine words to receive the blessings of Lord Vigneshwara.

Ebho Mathangajo, Hasthii, dandhii, kumbhii, karii, darii,
Sthambeeramoo, gajoo, garjoo, viradee, neekapoo, dwipaha
Dandavaloo, mahaakaayo, vaarana, kanjaroo, suraha
Mahaamrigaha, suurpakarnaha, saamajaha, sinduraha, kapiha,
Madavrinda, kushiikumbhaha, gundaalaha, shashtinaayanaha

71. Eight elephants in Hindu Mythology.

Chapter 10

Kothara-Kotharakolli-kotharamana

Shayya, thooyaavagaahashchalanamanugunam
Bheeshajam, dhuulivrishti:
Shaalaasthambhapraveesho, gruthagulasahitham
Bhoojanam puuladaanam
Nirvaanam thooyapaanam thilasahithamidam
Bhoojanam chaaparaahnee
Bhaishajyam chaadha samveeshana mithidinacha-
Ryaa gajaanaam krameena.
(*Mathangaleela*, ekadasaadhikaram, Slokam 8, Ardhavedi Vyakhyanam, Cheruvalli Narayanan Namboothiri)

Sleeping, bathing in rivers, proper exercises by movements
Giving necessary medicines, mud bathing
Chaining down in the crate,
food with ghee and jaggery and then grass bundles
Bathing, drinking of water, food with sesame seeds,
medicine in the evening,
Lying down to sleep-are the daily routine of elephants.
(Trans. Poornima G.)

In the book with interpretations that was published by the Thiruvithamcore (Travancore) University in 1942, constitutes certain values for regulation: There should be water (for drinking) placed near the pole where the elephant is chained, mahouts should walk behind the elephant, required medicines should be provided, enough sand should be provided for the elephant's sand-bath. In the elephant crate, the elephants should be fed with rice mixed with ghee and jaggery, elephants should also be given the required medicines, enough water to drink, a mixture of oil, medicine with rice should be given in the evenings and make sure that the elephants can stand comfortably in the crate. These are the routine care instructions. (These lines will help in understanding how language interpretation was, about 70 years ago).

From what I know, the foremost elephant owner would have been the member of Kotharamana. For the past 3-4 centuries, the lord-family had elephants all the time. Just one aspersion, though. Recently, for 3-4 days, the lord in Kotharamana did not possess any elephants, a short interval between an elephant sold and another bought. People in Kotharamana are not elephant-traders. Now, times have changed. If someone offers a good price, they would sell. Not for a huge margin of profit. No one can say when life of creatures will move out of them. In the ancient days, no one bought animals for selling. No one used to sell cows that have given birth 8-10 times. Grass and water were plenty. They might die a natural death. Now, depending on the price of their meat, cows and goats are sold. They go straight to the abattoir. ("Abattoir" is a rhetoric. Most of it is done on the roadside with the cover of a single coconut leaf. The skinned animals will be tied on the roadside. There are no prohibitions for the hanging decorations of meat on the highways.)

Until recently, elephants were not a trading "material." Never ever for the people of Kotharamana. They always need elephant in their homes. And they always had. Kothara was the name of the place. The complete name of the place was Kotharakkurissy. The family name was Veengaattoor. This name can be seen only in the legal documents. Many family-names of the lords are known after their place names. Desamangalam and Kuramaathoor are such names. There are also places that became famous because of family names. There are places that are known for cruel things. Like, Changuvetti (literal meaning, chopping off the heart) is a place name. Toponymy scholars have mentioned this. Most of them are known by the local deities. Nowadays, even place names are being modernized.

The relationship between the elephant and the owner is a mixture of love and fondness. The owner definitely loves the elephant. The elephant will love the owner as he provides food to it. But he should not resort to giving the elephant hard work. This is not based on fear but love. The elephant does not like to do hard work. The reason why it does is its fear. The spear in the mahout's hand. Repeated brutal beatings. When the elephant gets one on his *thavalakkuzhi*[72], he/she will obey.

There are cases where elephants that have not even been beaten with the midrib of a coconut leaf and have been fed daily with jaggery[73], coconut, banana and sugarcane have killed their owners. Most of them, by accident, for not knowing the situation of the elephants. Whatever said, elephant is a wild animal! One should be careful. Revenge and memory of elephants are strong, long-lasting. I remember an experiential story that I happened to read in *Bhavan's Journal* or *Reader's Digest* 10-15 years go. I do not exactly remember the source or the period of its publication. The story was the affidavit of a forest officer who was a witness to the incident. On the ground floor of the office where he worked, an isolated elephant was spotted. The elephant

72. Literally, the frog-hole. This part of elephant's body is the curve of the inner fold of the front legs.

73. It is a solidified sugarcane concentrate which is unprocessed and commonly used instead of crystallized sugar. In Kerala, sweets and porridges are traditionally made of jaggery.

had destroyed the cultivation. They made sounds by drumming tin boxes and throwing crackers to shoo the elephant away. But the elephant returned. For all of these, the officer took the lead. He became angrier at the elephant. He went up to a treehouse (or may be on top of a tree) so that when the elephant arrived, he could harm it. After days, the opportunity came for him to retaliate. Two flambeaus made of dry coconut spadix, a chain made of coconut leaves and tied with tyre pieces inside it. When the elephant was just below the tree, he lit both of these and put on its body. The lighted chain fell on the spine of the elephant and burned both the sides of the spine. The elephant could not shake it off its body as the melting tyre pieces stuck on its skin. In between, the officer sat on the top of the tree and scolded the elephant. Grumbling and moaning at the tree, the elephant ran, it would have dipped in a stream to put off the fire. The story ends.

Years passed by. An elephant was frequently spotted near the same forest office, situated within the forest boundaries. The bull-elephant had burned-marks on both its sides. He goes around the forest-office and disappears. It did not harm anyone. He screams lifting his trunk. Experienced people opined that he was searching for the forest officer–the person who burned the elephant's body–in the premises of the office. Our friend had once "tied the sacred thread around[74] the elephant's body" with burning tyre.

After years, the same forest officer returned to the office for some reason. He stayed in the same building. One-week-long stay. To attend to his responsibility, he went out of the building. His colleagues reminded him: "Sir, be careful. The old bull-elephant is around. He does not damage the cultivation nowadays, but…"

74. Referring to the circle of scar across the body of the elephant.

"Nothing to worry about. It is more than 30 years that I am here in the forest. He will not destroy the cultivation again. He will remember what he got from me, until his death."

"Sir, that's what we are worried about. He will remember you until his death."

"Yes! I will be careful. I will not go far. Moreover, it is afternoon right!"

While saying that he started walking out of the office. After he had walked for about two kilometres, an elephant appeared behind a tree. With his huge tusks he moved his head left to right. Grass grown on his back. He lifted his trunk, angry, and smelt the officer. The officer ran for his life. He somehow managed to climb up a huge tree. The elephant came near the tree, began striking it. He tried several times, but the tree wouldn't fall. The elephant looked up and waited at the foot of the tree for the officer to get down. Gathering great courage, he sat on the tree looking at the elephant raging for revenge. Time passed by. A she-elephant arrived from the forest, with a romantic smile. She came closer, touched and brushed him with her trunk. They whispered something. She was asked to watch over and he left for something. The officer immediately tried to get down the tree. Seeing this the she-elephant trumpeted with her curled trunk. She thrashed the tree and it was about to fall. By this time, the he-elephant returned. His trunk filled with water. He poured the water under the foot of the tree. Then, hit the tree with its head to uproot it. He continued to do this. The man who was sitting on top of the tree had 30 years of experience with the forest. He knew the elephant-mind. He calculated the time the elephant took to fetch the water. He decided to get down and run during this time. But the problem was the she-elephant was keeping a watch over the officer. But she does not have any enmity towards him and does not want to take any revenge.

Slowly, she began moving away from the tree, trying to find some grass. But before he returns, she has to get back to the foot of the tree. That's it. The time has come for his calculations were right. Exact. The tree is about to fall. If both the elephants try smashing the tree, it will fall. When the elephant had gone to get water, the forester got down and ran. She didn't notice. He returned. Tried to push the tree down. Finally, the tree fell. With the contentment of achieving the mission, the elephant roared aloud. He carefully searched for the man on the tree. The man who hurt him brutally wasn't there. He could not control his anger. He went closer to her. Would have mumbled something. He walked 10 feet backwards and mauled her hard and deep!! Her stomach burst opened; she fell. The dishonest lover was crushed under his foot.

This is the story. Elephants are intelligent. Elephants can communicate from about 20 *naazhikas*[75]. They can gauge the situations. An elephant can communicate to another elephant from one festival ground to a nearby one. They sniff and smell in about 3 *naazhikas*. The elephant knows his/her mahout by the sound of his voice. Through smell as well. Where humans live, the smells of liquor, nicotine, petrol and diesel create confusion in elephants. It is difficult to understand the exact smells. It is difficult to identify the mahout. Like the elephant identifies the body smells of the mahout and his family members, the mahout can identify the smells of the elephants as well. The situation of musth in elephants is best to be identified though its smell says the Rishi. Smell is more accurate than vision.

Sapthachadaambhoojasamaanagandhaha
Krudthahasadaa kumkumavarna daanaha

75. A measure of time equal to 24 minutes.

Aachoodithoo hasthiradhaashwasankha-
Naasaaditho gandhaparaamavasthaam.

(*Mathangaleela.* Madabhedaniroopanam, Shlokam 15, Cheruvalli Narayanan Namboothiri, Ardhadevi Vyakhyanam)

Those elephants with the smell of devil-tree[76] and lotus,
Always aggressive,
oozing out saffron (kumkumam[77]) coloured temporin[78] secretion,
Driving away other elephants, chariots and horses
And with strong scent, can be said to be in the state of musth.
(Trans. Poornima G.)

There is proof for traditional elephant-owners and mahouts to have made note of these conditions. Proof is from experience. Self-experience and the experience of others. Old people's (reference to mahout and owner) knowledge is traditional. The owner who knows the names of his father, grandfather and four great grandfathers are truly traditional. Even before that the family would have owned elephants and there would be mahouts whose brothers and uncles were elephant-people. Those people experienced the smell of elephants from the time they were born. Especially, people in Kotharamana.

Padmanabhan, who was known throughout Kerala by the name Kotharakolli, was also known as a calm elephant. But

76. *Alstonia scholaris* is commonly called blackboard tree or devil's tree. The plant flowers at night and is considered the abode of *yakshis* (she-devils). Various parts of the plant are used in *Ayurveda*.

77. Kunkumam or Sindoor (red in colour) is the auspicious vermilion on Devi's forehead. Traditionally, they were made of organic ingredients.

78. The secretion called temporin is secreted by temporal glands during musth.

kolli was a murderer who killed three people. This happened during the musth season. Padmanabhan, a half-tailed elephant, is usually known for his good behaviour during processions. He was nick-named kolli (a small stick) because of his half-tail which resembled a small stick. It is strange that a graceful elephant named Padmanabhan was known as kolli. (Imagine, a splay-legged elephant was called Swasti[79]). There were two other elephants along with this lord of grace—Balakrishnan and Chandrasekaran. Many temple festivals were conducted with these three. Balakrishnan died in an accident. Quite painful as well. In 1964 during *Vrichikam* (scorpio) he was taken on a procession for *Niramaala*[80]. The festival took place at the doorsteps of Kotharamana, at their family temple. It is doubtful if the musth fluid of the elephant had actually dried. While he returned from the Poomulli temple, the fluid was not seen outside but wouldn't have dried inside. He began quarrelling while at the temple. According to the instruction of the elder of Kotharamana, all the three elephants were brought to the holy space and the gate was closed. By that time, the elephant felled the flagstaff of the temple. He pierced the sacrifice slab. The rock slab broke. The first mahout tried his best to chain the violent elephant. The elephant turned back and shook the pyramid structure of the temple. The door broke and fell. The mad elephant came out of the temple. On his way, he destroyed everything, one by one. There was a huge wood in the yard that he split open. A piece of wood hitched up between the tusks. He tried to shake it off but failed. The angry elephant clobbered everything that he saw, with his trunk. Every strike brought the piece of wood stronger and closer to his head. His tusks broke and were

---

79. Swasti, a Sanskrit word, means source of all auspiciousness, blessing, welfare, fortune and prosperity.

80. Niramaala is a peculiar festival of the Hindus.

falling apart. He bled profusely. By then the mahouts who came from Guruvayoor beat and captured him. Carpenters came and removed the wood that got struck between the tusks. Balakrishnan was weak by then as he bled copiously due to the injury at the foot of the tusks and the tortures that he experienced in the process. After a day, the great majesty returned to heaven. Never heard of such a tragedy. Never happened later nor would ever happen in future.

Kotharakolli and Chandrasekharan lived for some more years. Even today, there are elephants in the family. Kotharakurissi Veengaattuuru was always an elephant-family. There are evidences to prove that Kothara Veengaattuuru Mana reared elephants from 1832. In the biography of Pazhanji Palli Muthappan, I have seen a short chapter on Eldo Mar Bassalios who was buried in Kothamangalam, which mentions the elephants.

Chapter 11

Anubhavam

(Experience)

There are many exalted stories about the love-revenge of elephants. Traditional veterinary science does not approve of all these. When compared to the body, an elephant's head is bigger. But light-weighted. The weight of the brain is one by 500th of the body. How about humans! One by 50th of the human body. When compared to the body, elephant's brain is under-developed, says science. So, most of the reverential elephant stories that we narrate are pure poetry, people would say. People who have experience do not lie. About 50 years ago, these were children's stories. Such stories were removed when education reformation took place in the State.

Once upon a time, there was an elephant. He was the Ganapathi of the temple. He lived within the temple premises. He lived happily eating offerings—rice, sweet porridge and red bananas. The elephant belongs to the deity. The temple goers also offer food. After eating, the elephant will shake his head. With affection, he murmurs. He was taken to a nearby river for bathing. River means a stream. On its way to the river, a tailor offers some food daily. Some jaggery. A mango. A jackfruit piece. Some things like that. Because of this routine, the elephant stops when he goes that way. He will make a sound to alert the tailor. He will extend his trunk. The tailor keeps something to eat on the trunk. One day the tailor thought he will do something mischievous. As always, the elephant stopped in front of the shop and extended its trunk. The tailor poked the trunk with a needle. As he poked on a sensitive area of the trunk, the elephant screamed and moved back. The tailor began laughing aloud. The elephant did not forget the pain. After his bath in the river, while returning, he stopped at the shop for some time. Then, he splashed the water that he carried in his trunk, quite forcefully, into the shop. The new clothes that people had given to stitch got wet. The elephant walked away as if he didn't know anything.

This is the story. An elephant will never forget people who hurt him/her. Also, people who love. There could be likes and dislikes with all animals who associate with humans. They keep the love and hate in their memories. I have heard the story of an elephant taking revenge on a person who fed coconut shell along with coconut meat. The elephant searched and found the person in a by-pass road and crushed him. There are stories of hostility that an elephant remembered for over 15 years. A single bull-elephant was spotted several times near the forest of Thirunelli on the way to Pakshipathaalam[81]. He waited there for the person who burnt his skin. This is my own experience as well.

Animals have an eternal fear for fire. Except for humans, all animals fear fire. Humans also fear. Since humans learned to put off the fire, they have overcome their fear. This was the great result of learning how to use fire when compared to the primal humans who knew only forest fire and lightening sparks.

Everyone knows, if an elephant quarrels in a festival ground, it does not run forward. Not because of the loud music played by the percussions and the wind. *Kuthu vilakku*[82] is a row of hand lamps which might have one, two, three, five and sometimes seven branches. At night, if there is a row of hand lamps in the front, no elephants will go forward crossing it. The farmers are

---

81. Pakshipathaalam is a mountainous landscape (a bird sanctuary now) in Wayanad District of Kerala.

82. Multi-wicked standing brass lamps.

aware of elephant's fear for fire. Mountainous people also know it. When elephants destroy their cultivation, they throw lighted flambeaus made of coconut leaves. Sitting in a treehouse, they tie these coconut leaves on both the sides of a metal rod that is chest-long and throw it on the elephant. The elephant might not be able to shake it off its body. The elephant experiences intense pain burning its back. The elephant in Thirunelli forest was walking around roaring as it was undergoing this pain. But he did not hurt anyone. He knows his enemy. When some of us were returning from Pakshipathaalam, we travelled through the side of River Kalindi. He did not hurt us. He didn't even notice us. My friends were about to run seeing the elephant. I stood there! Everyone mistook Madambu for an elephant expert. The elephant cannot do anything to him, they thought. That was not the truth. First of all, I was unable to run. Second, a wild elephant can run 30 miles per hour. Third, there were bamboo clusters all over the banks of the river!! However, he walked all the way to Thirunelli. He walked to the foot of the treehouse where his body was once burnt. We too walked. We decided to stay in the same treehouse that night.

For many years, the elephant walked through these places, it is said. Fearing the advancing elephant, two or three people ran and fell into the water canal. Got injured. One day, the elephant found the farmer who burned his back. Luckily, he fell into a sewage channel and saved his life from the chasing elephant. The elephant tried poking him out. But couldn't. Just think of the situation! A person, two meters below the tusk, he would have seen death face to face! The elephant waiting to maul him to death. Sheer luck. By then many people gathered. The elephant retreated. If the he-elephant was unable to fulfil his revenge, it is believed that his lover, the she-elephant, would do it for him. I narrated the story of a similar situation in a previous chapter where the he-elephant kills his lover for negligence of her duty.

This is how elephant-revenge works! Even though the brain is 1/500th of the weight of the elephant body, there is space for vendetta, anger, likeness, love, revenge, caring attitude and lust within it.

Not only anger and revenge, but they also possess love-friendships. Love that never withers in due time. Every day after the bath, the mother in the family gives a rice-ball. The elephant was 5-5.5 feet in height. The mother opens the tower-door (*gopuravaathil*) of the house (*naalukettu*) and gives sweets to the elephant. The elephant extends his head inside the door to munch the snack. Time flew. They sold the elephant-child. After 10-15 years, while the elephant was passing by the place, went straight into the house premises. Without listening to the instructions of the mahouts he went near the tower-door of the house and extended his head into the veranda! Poor thing! He did not realise how big he was. The log that held the roof also lifted along with the elephant's head. The corner of the house fell. But the elephant did not withdraw. Hearing the sounds of the arrival of the elephant, the mother came with sweet porridge and pickled mango. She sat down. The elephant lowered his lower lips, as if it was touching the floor! That's an elephant! Every elephant-owner might have such stories to share. This is not a contemporary story. Nowadays, I hear that even the elephant owners help in hurting the elephant. They like to sedate the elephant. The food and water given to the elephant are not normal but acidic, the elephant becomes weak and thus will not undergo musth. Four people stand around the elephant, beat and poke it to make it weak and tired. There are also techniques with heavy knives and axes.

I began with the elephant's fear for fire. In the game of chess, elephant is a chief defence, a fort and a tool for attack. The strongest army is the elephant-army. Yet, there are wars that have been lost because of elephants. The opponents who knew the psychology of elephants used fire. The elephants which turned back fearing the fire destroyed their own army. The elephant-army was divided. The entire army ran for their life in fear. As the elephant is capable of destroying (removing) the enemy, elephants were called *vaaranam*[83]. But the same reason is the cause of the failure of the army as well.

An important synonym of elephant is "*vaaranam*." A word having the same or nearly the same meaning as another in the same language is called a synonym, says dictionary. Generally, the denotation is correct. But if analysed logically, the word *vaaranam* cannot be considered a synonym for elephant. Nature is the reason. *Mathangaleela* has clearly given a rationale for the synonyms of elephant.

Elephant names were formed, respectively. Because the elephants travel from one place to another, they are called *gamanam*; *naagam*, because during special occasions they win (*jayikkuka*, meaning "to win"), they are called *gajam*; because the elephant was born out of the hand (*hastham*, meaning "hand") of Brahma, he is called *hasthi*; because they destroy (*vaaranam*, meaning "to avoid") the army of the enemy, they are called *vaaranam*; because lessons are taught through torture (*mardanam*, meaning "torture"), they are called *maathangam*; because they are much thirsty (*daaham*, meaning "thurst"), they are called *kunjaram*; because of the swiftness of the legs (*paadam*, meaning "legs") and their likings for lotus (*thaamara*, meaning, "lotus"), they are called *padmi*; because they drink with their trunk (*thumbi*, meaning "trunk") and mouth (*vaaya*, meaning "mouth"), they are called *dweepam*.

(*Mathangaleela*, Page 42, Brahmasri Charuvalli Narayanan Namboothiri's Ardhavedi translation)

In *Amarakosham*[84], one can see 15 synonyms of elephant and in *Vyjayanthee Kosham*, 28. All the words have different

83. The literal meaning of the word is to eliminate.

84. Amarakosham is a Sanskrit thesaurus written by the poet, Amarasimha. Read more about the text here: https://aksharasadhana.com/2019/05/20/introduction-to-amarakosham/

meanings. Generally, all these words mean elephant. But now one can decide which words best suit the context.

According to modern life-science, there are 352 kinds of elephants. This means: "an organism which has been created with the upper lip from its head and which extends like a hollow pipe that transformed to a trunk." The scientific name is Proboscidea. Now, there are only African and Asian elephants. They are divided into three kinds: Dinotherioidea, Elephantoidea and Maeritherioidea. (I have quoted the scientific details from Dr. K. C. Panickar's scientific monograph titled *Aana: Kadhayum Karyavum* [Elephant: Myth and Truth]).

Our scientific books prescribe to swallow medicines by chanting sacred shlokams. It is merely a material belief. A few blind beliefs are also practiced ... Place an antlion in a red banana and feed the elephant for 40 days. The elephant will thereafter not quarrel.

"*Lavana rishi ha pangthi chandaha swaahaadeevii devathaa. Urathirunthapaathiyil veluthezhuntha vellappamaatham paralthanna hooree marannu thane marannu ennee ninantha ennadikkil vasamaayirikka swaaha, madanee manapriyee swaaha.*"[85]

"Chant these shlokas 12,000 times and feed salt; pink salt[86] or white salt. This will definitely influence the elephant."

Why don't you try it with the elephant?

85. This is a meaningless shloka, which combines some meaningless words in Sanskrit and Tamil. These words satirise the perspectives of humans that elephants should be medicated for the benefit of humans.

86. Pink salt is also known as Himalayan rock salt.

Glossary

Arattupuzha Pooram is the oldest temple festival of India known for its magnitude and grandeur. This is a seven-day festival with rituals, devotion and grand music. The fireworks and the percussion music are the highlights of the festival. Arattupuzha Sree Shastha Temple is situated in Thrissur district of Kerala State.

Dandu (Goad) in Malayalam is a tool employed by mahouts in the handling and training of elephants. Dandu is also known as bull-hook or ankus.

Gajashasthram (Elephantology) is the art and craft of maintaining and treating elephants. This work is believed to be written by Sivamara, the Second, in South Karnataka in 830 A.D.

Illam is the name of a Namboothiri's (Brahmin) house, where he is born.

Kottaram Sankunni (1855-1937) was a Malayalam writer known for his classic work *Aitheehyamala*, a collection of legendary stories gathered from various parts of Kerala.

Moksham is the freedom that one attains after physical death. Indian religions consider this state of being as a rebirth or completeness of self.

Musth is a fluid secretion which is produced by bull-elephants to attract she-elephants for mating. This is the production of a reproductive hormone in the body of he-elephants. The elephant becomes aggressive and mischievous during this time. During this time, the elephant produces a secretion on both the sides of its head. It also steadily discharges secretions through its genitals.

Naalukettu describes the structure of a mana or *illam*. *Naalukettu* (literally, four-structured) is divided into four sections—in the north, south, east and west. A *naalukettu* has one courtyard. There are also *ettukettu* (eight-structured) and *pathinaarukettu* (sixteen-structured). Several generations of matrilineal families lived in *naalukettu*.

Onam is an annual harvest festival celebrated by people in the State of Kerala. This is also believed to celebrate the arrival of the just King Mahabali, who is allowed to visit his kingdom once in a year.

Pazhani Kshethram: Arulmigu Dhandayuthapani Swami Temple is situated in the city of Palani in Dindugal District in Tamil Nadu State.

Rasika is the ultimate aesthete. A rasika has knowledge of art and music, might not be a performer, but has in-depth knowledge of the art, particularly fine arts.

Sreeraman Chovvalloor Krishnankutty is a Malayalam writer who has written works such as *Madhaviyamma muthal Madhavikutty Vare* [From Madhaviamma to Madhavikutty], *Ente Preeyappetta Ormakal* [My Dear Memories] and *Neerathe Pootha Kanikonna* [The Golden Shower Flowers that Bloomed Early].

Sreerangam is a river-island-city in the district of Tiruchirappalli in the State of Tamil Nadu. From Chengallooru, Sreerangam is about 320 kilometres.

Vallathol Narayana Menon (1878-1958), popularly known as Mahakavi (Great poet) Vallathol was a poet and a social reformer. He wrote against caste and atrocities against the lower castes. He was a Gandhian who took efforts in revitalizing Kathakali and contributed in setting up **Kerala Kalamandalam** (a University of Art and Culture that offers training in classical dance, music and theatre forms).

Vedas are the oldest known scriptures of Hinduism composed in Sanskrit. There are four *Vedas*, *The Rig Veda*, *The Yajurveda*, *The Samaveda* and The *Atharvaveda*.

VKN, Vadakke Koottala Narayanankutty Nair, a.k.a. VKN (1929-2004) was a Malayalam writer known for his satirical novels and short stories.

About the Translators

Rayson K. Alex is Associate Professor at the Department of Humanities and Social Sciences, Birla Institute of Technology and Science Pilani, K. K. Birla Goa Campus, Goa. He is the secretary of tiNai (formerly, Organisation for Studies in Literature and Environment-India [OSLE-India]), a pioneering academic body in India promoting the area of ecocriticism. He is one of the editors of *Essays in Ecocriticism* (Sarup and Sons, New Delhi; 2007), *Culture and Media: Ecocritical Explorations* (Cambridge Scholars Publishing, UK, 2014), *Ecodocumentaries: Critical Essays* (Palgrave Macmillan, USA, 2016) and *Ecocultural Ethics: Critical Essays* (Lexington Books, USA, 2017), *Anthropocene Ecologies of Food: Notes from the Global South and Beyond* (Routledge, USA, 2022), and *Desertscapes in the Global South and Beyond: Anthropocene Naturecultures* (Routledge, USA, 2023). He has directed/co-directed a few ethnographic video-documentaries of which the popular ones are *The Story of Mudugar, Narikuravar* (Life of a gypsy community in Tamil Nadu), *Jenukurubar* (Life of a tribal community in Karnataka), *Learning from Jenukurubar* and *Nila Paranjathu* (What the Nila Said—art forms of the communities living on the banks of river Nila in Kerala). He was a Fulbright (Academic and Professional Excellence Award - Teaching and Research) fellow to Western Washington University (2022-23). He is the Founder and co-Director of tiNai Ecofilm Festival (www.teff.in).

Poornima G., Ph.D., is Assistant Professor at the Department of Sanskrit Sahitya at the Sree Sankaracharya University of Sanskrit (Regional Campus), Ettumanoor, Kottayam, Kerala State.